PACIFIC AIR RACE

PACIFIC AIR RACE

Robert H. Scheppler

SMITHSONIAN INSTITUTION PRESS
WASHINGTON, D.C.
LONDON

Copyright © 1988 by the Smithsonian Institution
All rights reserved

Edited by Jan Danis

Cover: Takeoff of *Oklahoma* (detail). Photo by Dole Co.

Library of Congress Cataloging-in-Publication Data
Scheppler, Robert H., 1921–
    Pacific air race.

    Bibliography: p.
    Includes index.
    1. Transpacific flights—History. I. Title.
TL531.S34   1988   629.13′091   87-28847
ISBN 0-87474-832-1

∞ The paper used in this publication
meets the minimum requirements of the
American National Standard for
Permanence of Paper for Printed Library
Materials Z39.48-1984.

CONTENTS

ACKNOWLEDGMENTS   vii
PROLOGUE   1

1	THE DAY	3
2	ON THE MARK	8
3	BEATING THE GUN	15
4	THE RULES	22
5	THE LINEUP	28
6	THE MAD SCRAMBLE	54
7	HAWAII PREPARES	64
8	GET SET	68
9	GO	74
10	ACROSS THE PACIFIC	80
11	THE FINISH	88
12	MEANWHILE, BACK AT THE FIELD	94
13	SEARCH AND FAILURE	102

14	*DALLAS SPIRIT* TO THE RESCUE	106
15	THE SEARCH CONTINUES	111
16	RESULTS	117

APPENDIX: AIRCRAFT SPECIFICATIONS   121

NOTES   137

SELECT BIBLIOGRAPHY   141

INDEX   144

ACKNOWLEDGMENTS

The hardest part of writing any book has to be the section titled "Acknowledgments." Over the years so many individuals have helped me to tell the story of the Pacific Air Race that I cannot even attempt to list them all for fear of overlooking someone. Between us I believe we have been able to tell the true story of the race and put to rest some of the accusations and falsehoods concerning it that have surfaced over the years. It was a glorious event and, though surrounded by tragedy, it still deserves a high position in the comparatively short history of aviation.

My sincere thank you goes to all those people I have talked to, corresponded with, and borrowed from, with an additional special thank you to my family.

PROLOGUE

In the remote town of Bartlesville, Oklahoma, you can find a small museum called Woolaroc. To most visitors, in fact to most Americans, this name means little. Browsing among the exhibits you will soon note that each depicts the history of the land of Oklahoma. But in one room there is an exhibit strangely out of place, out of keeping with the rest. It is an airplane. Not a big, beautiful, modern jet—not a huge, four-engine dinosaur of the skies, but a small, single-engine, wire, wood, and fabric airplane. Its bright blue fuselage and orange wings have been recently restored in their original colors, and the name *Woolaroc* in big white letters adorns the fuselage. Few visitors recognize it, in fact some hardly notice it. But if airplanes had memories this one could fill a book. For this is THE *Woolaroc*, named for the woods, the lakes, and the rocks, the same *Woolaroc* that early in its career had the entire world waiting for word of its deeds.

In a large way this airplane and its crew were responsible for the routine daily flights across the Pacific Ocean, the thousands of business people and pleasure-seekers who fly from the continental United States to Hawaii, the Philippines, and the Orient every day of the year.

Seventy-five thousand people watched the *Woolaroc* take off on its flight to glory from California to Hawaii and fifty thousand watched it land, but few today have any memory of that great event. It happened in 1927, more than half a century, almost a lifetime ago. After reading the plaque in front of the *Woolaroc* many children ask "What's so great about flying to Hawaii? Is there any other way to go?"

The story of the *Woolaroc* needs retelling in this jet age, because without her and many more that followed her trail there would be no jet age.

1

THE DAY

The date was 16 August 1927. The place—Oakland, California. The day was dawning much like other typical beautiful California days with the sun glowing like a red hot coal through the early morning haze and fog. Early risers felt the first trace of a breeze, and the weatherman predicted by midmorning the Oakland area would be enjoying another lazy summer day.

But first impressions were deceiving. This would not be a typical day nor would it be termed lazy in the Oakland–San Francisco area. For even at dawn there was an abnormal hum of activity, a movement of machines and a gathering of people with the hub of activities centered on the Oakland Airport, across the bay from San Francisco. A few aircraft engines were being started over and over, apparently being adjusted to a fine degree. People were starting to congregate in groups around the various airplanes parked at the edge of the field, and a tense air of expectancy was beginning to be felt by all. And rightly so, for this day was to live forever in the memory of every member of the crowd, the most advertised event in the history of aviation was scheduled to begin—the Pacific Air Race to Hawaii, sponsored by James D. Dole, president of the Hawaiian Pineapple Company.

In glancing over the rapidly forming crowd and noting a lineup of nine airplanes in various stages of preparation for flight, each surrounded by a small group of sweating mechanics and spectators, one would find it hard to believe that only three short months before no one had even thought of a Pacific Air Race.

Flying across oceans was not exactly a new pastime in 1927, but it still was not an everyday affair. In the years immediately after World War I the eyes of the aeronautical world were focused on the Atlantic Ocean, primarily because of the strong economic ties between Europe and America. Another factor was the distances involved were almost within the realm of possibility for air travel. With proper planning it was possible to fly an approximate great circle course from the United States to Europe making use of the various land masses such as Newfoundland, Greenland, Iceland, and the northwestern portions of the European continent to minimize the overwater portion of the crossing. Even though some of the land masses to be crossed were as dangerous as the open seas to a flier forced down, flying over land provided a limited sense of security.

As early as 1873 man began attempting to cross the Atlantic by air. On 7 October of that year William H. Donaldson, Alfred Ford, and George A. Lunt, of the New York *Daily Graphic*, left Brooklyn, New York, in a balloon (naturally called *Graphic*) in an attempt to cross the Atlantic. They only reached New Canaan, Connecticut, before landing, but their trip is certainly a noteworthy starting point in a long line of attempted ocean crossings.

On 15 October 1910 Walter Wellman, journalist and explorer, and his crew of five left Atlantic City, New Jersey, in an airship named *America*. The ship was 228 feet in length, equipped with two 80-horsepower engines and capable of cruising at a speed of 20 miles per hour. Even with luck it would take six days to reach Europe. They covered approximately 800 miles before abandoning the airship in favor of the lifeboat they carried. By sheer luck they were rescued by the steamer *Trent*.

There were no further attempts for a few years due to World War I, but the year 1919 was filled with both successful and unsuccessful attempts. On 18 May Harry C. Hawker and McKenzie Grieve left St. Johns, Newfoundland, in a Sopwith biplane and flew 1,200 miles in 14 1/2 hours before descending alongside a steamer and being rescued.

Later on the same day, Capt. F. P. Raynham and C. W. F. Morgan, in a Martinsyde airplane, attempted to follow Hawker and Grieve from the same field but damaged their aircraft during preparation for the takeoff.

The first successful flight across the Atlantic was achieved by the U.S. Navy sponsored Curtiss flying boat, NC–4, in May 1919. Originally four planes and a Navy semirigid blimp were to have made the flight. Mechanical troubles and a minor accident eliminated one plane and the blimp. Three planes started from Newfoundland but only the NC–4 completed the crossing by air. The actual flight from Newfoundland to Horta on the isle of Fayal was completed on 16 and 17 May. Leaving Horta on 20 May, the NC–4 continued to Porta Delgada and from there to Lisbon, Portugal, on 27 May. The final leg was completed to Plymouth, England, on 30 May 1919. The NC–4 was flown across the Atlantic by Lt. Cmdr. Albert C. Read, pilots Lt. Elmer Stone and Lt. Walter Hinton, Chief Engineer Lt. James Breese, radioman Ens. Herbert C. Rodd, and Chief Machinist Mate Eugene S. Rhodes.

The Day

Inspired by the success of the NC–4, on 22 May 1919 Raymond Orteig, New York hotel owner, offered a prize of 25,000 dollars to the first pilot to fly nonstop across the Atlantic Ocean either from Paris to New York or New York to Paris. This offer was somewhat premature, however, as the aircraft designers of 1919 were not yet capable of designing an aircraft for such a flight.

The NC–4 flight was followed very shortly by a crossing on 14 June 1919. Lt. Arthur W. Brown and Capt. John Alcock, R.A.F. fliers, in a converted Vickers Vimy bomber, again left from Newfoundland but crash-landed in Ireland. Neither Alcock nor Brown was hurt, and they could lay claim to the first nonstop flight between the two continents. They were showered with national honors and split a cash prize of 10,000 British pounds (about 50,000 dollars at that time).

A month later the R–34 carried thirty crewmen and one stowaway from East Fortune, Scotland, to Mitchell Field, Garden City, New York, a distance of 3,130 nautical miles. Within a few days the R–34 returned to England without any trouble. Yet this fantastic accomplishment between 2 July and 12 July 1919 has all but been forgotten. It should be mentioned that the R–34 was a British dirigible, but this does not detract in any way from the fantastic feat. Thus by the end of 1919 a total of thirty-nine persons had flown across the Atlantic, with thirty of them making a round trip.

No further serious attempts were made to span the Atlantic by air until 1924. In that year a group of Army fliers made a "Round the World" flight. They started with four planes but ended with only two. Their flight originated in Seattle on 6 April 1924 and ended back in Seattle on 28 September 1924. It took 175 days, including 375 hours and 11 minutes flying time. A total of 26,345 miles were covered, and portions of both the Atlantic and Pacific Oceans were crossed in a series of separate flights.

In 1925 the first serious attempt was made to cross the Pacific by air. On 31 August 1925 Cmdr. John Rodgers, Naval Aviator Number Two and Lt. Byron Connell, and radio operator Otis Stantz, plus two crewmen flew a Navy PN–9 flying boat 1,992 miles from San Pablo Bay, California, to a point a few hundred miles northeast of Hawaii. At this point, partly due to poor weather and partly due to poor navigation, they ran out of fuel and were forced to land. They successfully landed about 4:00 A.M. in the relatively calm sea. Though short of their destination of Hawaii, they had set a record for nonstop, heavier-than-air flight of 1,730 nautical miles. The aircraft was in good shape, and, being able Navy men, they rigged covering from the lower wing for a sail and used the floorboards for a rudder. In this way they sailed about 50 miles a day for eight days before being sighted about 10 miles from land at 4:30 P.M. on 10 September by the U.S submarine R–4. They accepted a tow for the last portion of their trip but insisted on beaching the PN–9 flying boat on the shore at the town of Nawilliwili on the island of Kauai.

Technically they had flown and sailed from California to Hawaii. The airplane was still in good shape and within a few weeks had been reconditioned and put into service on patrol duty in Hawaii.

Now the stage was set for the various overocean flights of 1927. Suddenly the prize of 25,000 dollars offered by Raymond Orteig for the first nonstop flight between New York and Paris appeared to be within reach. A mad scramble ensued among many of the prominent fliers of the day to obtain suitable aircraft and prepare for an Atlantic crossing. All thoughts of Pacific flights were forgotten by most of the flying fraternity.

In September 1926 Rene Fonck, a French flier, with three crewmen attempted to take off from New York for Paris. They were flying a Sikorsky twin-engine plane, but with the required fuel load and four people the plane was severely overloaded. A special set of wheels had been added to handle the increased weight, but one of the wheels collapsed during the takeoff roll, resulting in a fiery crash that only Fonck survived.

Other pilots and crew members, undaunted by Fonck's crash, began congregating at East Coast airports, primarily Roosevelt Field, New York, and Teterboro, New Jersey. On 26 April 1927 Lt. Cmdr. Noel Davis and Lt. Stanton Wooster crashed to their death while preparing their converted Keystone bomber for a Paris flight. On 8 May 1927 Capt. Charles Nungesser, a French World War I ace with forty-five victories, and Francis Coli, another French flier, disappeared on a trans-Atlantic flight. But on 20 and 21 May 1927 Charles Lindbergh made his famous New York–Paris flight and a new era of aviation was opened. The world went wild in its acclaim for Lindbergh, and caught up in this surge of hero worship was James D. Dole of Honolulu, Hawaii. Dole had never been a serious devotee of flying, but as president of the Hawaiian Pineapple Company, and a good businessman, he had always been quick to grasp an opportunity when offered. At the time of Lindbergh's flight Dole was visiting the mainland in California. He was extremely impressed with Lindbergh's achievement. As if by prearrangement two enterprising reporters of the Honolulu *Star Bulletin*, Riley Allen and Joe Farrington, sent a cable to Dole in San Francisco on 23 May.

IN VIEW LINDBERGH'S ATLANTIC FLIGHT PACIFIC REMAINS ONE GREAT AREA FOR CONQUEST AVIATION STOP SITUATION THIS MOMENT RIPE SOMEONE OFFER SUITABLE PRIZE NON STOP FLIGHT HAWAII STOP FROM ANGLE ADVERTISING ISLANDS AND YOURSELF WE BELIEVE EXCEPTIONAL OPPORTUNITY YOUR OFFER TWENTY FIVE THOUSAND DOLLAR PRIZE FOR THIS ACHIEVEMENT STOP PARTICULARLY IN VIEW YOUR NATIONAL PINEAPPLE ADVERTISING FEATURING YOUR NAME WE BELIEVE

YOU NOW TO DO THIS STOP PRIZE SHOULD BE KNOWN DOLE PRIZE STOP THIS WILL PUT YOUR NAME EVERY NEWSPAPER IN WORLD BESIDES GREAT CREDIT TERRITORY PINEAPPLE INDUSTRY STOP WE PREPARED COOPERATE EVERY POSSIBLE WAY STOP AWAIT ANXIOUSLY FAVORABLE REPLY ON WHICH WE WOULD LIKE FIRST ANNOUNCEMENT STOP APPRECIATE EARLY REPLY BY WIRE STOP NOT PUBLISHING ANYTHING UNTIL HEARING FROM YOU RILEY ALLEN JOE FARRINGTON STAR BULLETIN

It took Dole very little time to decide to back the California–Hawaii flight proposed by Allen and Farrington. He cabled the *Star Bulletin* his agreement and asked them to start making arrangements to announce the prize.

On Tuesday 24 May another cable was sent to San Francisco.

ANNOUNCING OFFER EXTRA WEDNESDAY MORNING STOP ASSOCIATED PRESS SENDING OUT STORY FOR RELEASE NINE MORNING SAN FRANCISCO TIME TO CATCH EVENING PAPERS ALL OVER COUNTRY STOP CONFIRMING DOLE DESIRE GIVE LINDBERGH CHANCE TO STIPULATE FLIGHT NOT BEFORE AUGUST 15 UNLESS LINDBERGH UNWISH COMPETE STOP ALSO SET LIMIT YEAR WITHIN OFFER GOOD STOP FURTHER CONDITIONS MAY BE SETTLED AFTER CONSULTATION AERONAUTIC OFFICIALS HERE AND WE ASSUME CERTAIN NATIONAL ASSOCIATION RULES MUST BE FOLLOWED STOP REGARDING DROPPING LETTER LANAI FEEL BEST SECURE EXPERT ADVISE WHETHER THIS DETOUR ENDANGER FLIERS MAKING HONOLULU HENCE NOT ANNOUNCING NOW STOP ARE STRESSING SPIRIT DOLE OFFER AND RESULTANT EMPHASIS HAWAII'S POSITION WORLD STOP SUGGEST RELAYING THIS TO DOLE WITH SUGGESTION HE FEEL FREE GIVE INTERVIEWS USE ALL OPPORTUNITIES PUBLICITY WHILE NEWS OF OFFER FRESH STOP ALLEN FARRINGTON

The reference to Lanai was due to a previous suggestion by Dole that the fliers drop an air-mail letter on the island of Lanai on their way to Honolulu. This island had recently been purchased by Dole and was being developed by the Hawaiian Pineapple Company. It was destined to become the largest pineapple producing area in the world, and at the time Dole was anxious to exploit it whenever possible.

The next day, Wednesday 25 May 1927, the Honolulu *Star Bulletin* published the short article that electrified the flying world and set the stage for the greatest air race of all time.

James D. Dole, believing that Charles A. Lindbergh's extraordinary feat in crossing the Atlantic is the forerunner of eventual trans-Pacific air transportation, offers $25,000 to the first flier and $10,000 to the second flier to cross from the North American continent to Honolulu in a non-stop flight within one year after the beginning August 12, 1927.

2

ON THE MARK

1927 promised to be a wonderful year. Tom Mix and his fabulous horse Tony were cleaning up the West each Saturday afternoon for the small fry. Pauline met and almost succumbed to a new peril each week, and in the evening Mary Pickford and Doug Fairbanks made every young girl's heart flutter and every young man show greater interest in young girls. The horrors of the past war were fading from memory, and the pulp magazine writers were creating new heroes of their own. Some heroes of the aerial battles over France were still making headlines, Eddie Rickenbacker and Billy Mitchell in the United States, Billy Bishop in Canada, and Nungesser in France. Air mail was no longer a stunt but a reality—if you had the ten cents for each half ounce. An occasional passenger, brave enough to buy a ticket to fly, rode on top of the mail sacks if there was enough space. This was the way it was in 1927 when James Dole first published his prize offer.

After seeing the excitement caused by the terse announcement of the Dole prize in newspapers throughout the world, the editor of the Honolulu *Star Bulletin* devoted most of the front page and many of the inner pages of the 25 May late edition to a discussion of the proposed race. The headline read "Three Planes Already In Race For James D. Dole's $25,000 Prizes." The editor did not elaborate on where the three planes were or who would fly them. Dole was quoted as stating his expressed wish that Charles Lindbergh, having already conquered the Atlantic, would have full opportunity to compete for the Dole prize. He specifically ruled that the race was not to start before 12 August, to allow Lindbergh ample time to enter if he so desired. Dole also intimated that the date for the start might be moved forward if Lindbergh made it known that he definitely did not wish to compete. Dole sent a personal invitation to Lindbergh, who at this time was still in Europe preparing to make his triumphal return to the United States. Lindbergh never did answer Dole's invitation nor did he ever seriously consider entering the race.

The 25 May late edition of the Honolulu *Star Bulletin* also stated that the Honolulu chapter of the National Aeronautics Association had been chosen by Dole to work out all details of the event and to prepare a complete set of rules covering both planes and pilots.

Many prominent Washington officials such as Hubert Work, secretary of the interior, Clarence Young, chief of the Air Relations Bureau of the Department of Commerce, and C. F. Shorey, chairman of the contest committee of the National Aeronautics Association, praised Dole's offer and assured the public that some intrepid fliers would rapidly complete the nonstop flight in the prescribed time.

Shorey elaborated further: "That offer will be snapped up in short order and it is a question of only a short time before a non-stop flight across the Pacific becomes a reality. I think you will soon hear of a prize offered by New York interests for a non-stop flight from Seattle to Japan."

As the excitement of Lindbergh's flight started to wane many people felt that the young unassuming man had performed the impossible with apparently little effort. It was only natural for the public to feel that any long-distance flight should be possible. As with any pioneering effort in a relatively new field such as aeronautics, the public failed to appreciate the hazards involved, the cost of preparation, the planning required, and the type of specialized equipment used. The average man felt that if the Atlantic could be conquered why not the Pacific. All you had to do was add enough gasoline and keep flying. Which was true. But little did the man on the street understand the problems involved to perform both these feats. Prevailing west to east headwinds, normal weather conditions over the Pacific, unreliability of both aircraft and engines, meager knowledge of aerial navigation, and lack of any form of aerial maps were a few of the nearly insurmountable hurdles that were not appreciated. Very few people knew that the manufacturer of the Wright J–5 engine used by Lindbergh and later by all of the Dole race pilots stated it had to be manually lubricated every 25 hours. No aircraft in use in 1927 was meant to fly more than four or five hours without some maintenance. Naturally most of these tasks were impossible to perform during flight, so any pilot flying long distances was literally on borrowed time.

Navigation up to 1927 was practically an unknown art in the aviation field. Lindbergh spent many long hours learning basic navigation while his plane was being built. Most pilots relied on the "iron compass," railroad tracks, which they followed to their destination. Radio directional aids were nonexistent. The best instruments in use were still subject to errors of 10 percent or more. When Lindbergh took off he was heading for a whole continent. The Dole pilots would be aiming at a speck of an island.

Very few fliers had been lost up to 1927 on ocean flights primarily because few flights of this type had been attempted. The large number of failures that were to follow in the late twenties and early thirties had not yet started to mount. Consequently the public expected more excitement, more heroes, more conquests. The World War had been over for almost ten years, and the country and the entire world were in an era of accelerating prosperity. After a slow period following the war, world trade and world travel began to increase by leaps and bounds. Americans were starting to show interest in far-off places such as Hawaii, Japan, and the South Seas. Improved methods of communication were opening up new areas of interest, and the time appeared ripe for the exploitation and bally-hoo of the Pacific Air Race. Naturally the newspapers made the most of it, and daily headlines concerning the race were in evidence in most of the nation's newspapers. Nowhere was this more noticeable than in Hawaii, especially Honolulu. Within 24 hours after the initial announcement newsmen all over the world were frantically interviewing prominent fliers of the day, assuming they would all have intentions of entering the Pacific Air Race. Some of the stories printed at the time are so amazing it appears that the interviews took place in the reporters' imaginations.

Clarence Chamberlain, noted flier, was in New York where he had been preparing for the Orteig prize won by Lindbergh. He was mentioned as a probable entrant flying his Bellanca monoplane, the *Columbia*. Commander Byrd, also in New York, was preparing to fly to Paris. He was quoted as seriously considering a Pacific flight.

Martin Jensen, a Honolulu pilot, announced his plans to fly alone from California to Hawaii. He said that he had long been planning the flight; with the added inducement of the Dole offer there was no doubt that he would try for it. Harvey Lemcke, another Honolulu resident and a former Navy flier, indicated he would be an entrant, but he refused to disclose the identity of his backers.

Louis Bleriot, Jr., son of the famed French pioneer flier, was reported to be planning to enter flying a French plane. The St. Louis businessmen who originally backed Lindbergh announced they would again invest their money if Lindbergh would consider entering the Pacific race. The Douglas Airplane Company of California stated they were negotiating with several persons concerning the building of aircraft for the race.

It appeared that within 24 hours of the original announcement a sufficient number of fliers were ready and willing to enter the contest, and a successful race seemed assured. Estimates indicated that a half-dozen to possibly two dozen fliers would be on hand for the starting date.

After the original announcement, the Honolulu *Star Bulletin* requested Dole to forward a statement that they could use as a followup. Dole responded with the following wire:

IN RESPONSE TO YOUR REQUEST FOR STATEMENT RELATIVE TO PRIZE OFFER ANNOUNCED TODAY THE FLIGHT OF CAPTAIN LINDBERGH IS AN EVIDENCE OF THE STARTLING PROGRESS BEING MADE IN AERONAUTICS STOP IT SEEMED OBVIOUS THAT A FLIGHT FROM THE MAINLAND TO HAWAII WAS NEXT IN ORDER AND THAT DEFINATE ACTION TO ENCOURAGE SUCH FLIGHT WOULD BE APPROPRIATE STOP UNTIL RECENTLY WHILE I HAVE LOOKED UPON AVIATION AS OF ULTIMATE ECONOMIC IMPORTANCE IT HAS TAKEN THE LINDBERGH CONQUEST OF THE ATLANTIC TO MAKE ME REALIZE THAT HAWAII IN PARTICULAR NEEDS TO HAVE THE FUTURE OF AVIATION BROUGHT NEARER TO THE PRESENT STOP CONSIDER THE HELP GIVEN TO HAWAII'S PROGRESS BY THE CABLE THE RADIO THE AUTOMOBILE AND TRUCK STOP WHAT WOULD WE DO WITHOUT THEM TODAY STOP THE CONTINUED ADVANCE IN AVIATION MAY MEAN WITHIN A FEW YEARS MAIL DELIVERED IN HONOLULU IN TWENTY HOURS FROM THE MAINLAND STOP IT MAY MEAN THAT IN CASE OF EMERGENCY THE BUSINESSMAN OR VISITOR CAN MAKE THE JOURNEY IN A DAY STOP I HOPE THAT THE REWARD NOW OFFERED MAY BRING THIS EVENTUALLY CLOSER STOP THIS OCCASSION SEEMED TO BE A FAVORABLE OPPORTUNITY TO BRING THE ISLANDS STILL NEARER TO THE PUBLIC EYE AT A MOMENT WHEN THE ENTIRE WORLD IS ON THE QUIVIVE DUE TO CAPTAIN LINDBERGH'S EXTRAORDINARY PERFORMANCE STOP THE PAPERS OVER HERE HAVE RECEIVED THE ANNOUNCEMENT WITH FRIENDLY ENTHUSIASM ESPECIALLY ON THE COAST WHILE DISPATCHES INDICATING BOTH INTEREST AND COOPERATION WERE RECEIVED FROM ST. LOUIS AND NEW YORK IN LESS THAN TWO HOURS AFTER NEWS OF THE OFFER WAS RELEASED STOP MUCH ACTIVITY APPEARS TO BE DEVELOPING TO INSURE A GOOD FIELD OF PROPERLY EQUIPPED CONTESTANTS FOR A FLIGHT THIS SUMMER STOP NO PRECAUTION CAN BE TOO GREAT TO SATISFY ALL WHO ARE SINCERELY INTERESTED IN THE PERMANENT DEVELOPMENT OF AVIATION STOP IT IS NATURAL FOR ALL OF US IN HAWAII AS WELL AS ALL FOLLOWERS OF AVIATION THE WORLD OVER TO HOPE THAT THIS CONTEST MAY BE DOUBLY SUCCESSFUL FIRST THAT IT MAY COST NO BRAVE MAN EITHER LIFE OR LIMB AND SECOND THAT THE CONTINENT AND HAWAII MAY BE LINKED BY AIRPLANE STOP I SHOULD BE GLAD TO SEE CAPTAIN LINDBERGH THE MAN FIRST TO MAKE THIS FLIGHT SUCCESSFULLY AND TO BE ABLE TO GREET HIM AT THE RODGERS AIRPORT IN HONOLULU STOP

JAMES D. DOLE

Dole was quite sincere in his efforts to advance the state of the science of aviation. He was also most interested in improving the status of the territory of Hawaii. This was partially based on his position as president of the world's largest pineapple-producing company but to an even greater extent on his sincere love for Hawaii. He had moved to the islands shortly after graduating from Harvard in 1899. By 1903 he acquired a small cannery, which he developed into the Hawaiian Pineapple Company. He felt that any good publicity that could be obtained for Hawaii would eventually improve it commercially and also help publicize it as a vacation paradise. James Dole was so convinced of this and so sincere in his love for the islands that he provided the funds for the prizes from his own personal finances, not the Hawaiian Pineapple Company's.

The actual choice of the date for the race was apparently based on several events. Dole definitely hoped to have Lindbergh compete in the race and planned the date accordingly. Also 12 August was the anniversary of the date Hawaii became a territory of the United States in 1898. It had been reported there would be a full moon that night, which should help the fliers, and the peak of the pineapple harvest would be past, allowing the Hawaiian Pineapple Company employees to have time off to celebrate the fliers' arrival. What some writers overlook is that at the time of the announcement neither Dole nor anyone else expected a large group of fliers to be ready on the proposed date. For this reason he set a one-year completion time on his offer.

Dole's attempt to publicize Hawaii and aviation started immediately to produce results. Many prominent Hawaiian people released statements praising Dole for his offer and expressing opinions concerning the many benefits that would result both for aviation and the territory of Hawaii. W. R. Farrington, governor of Hawaii, R. C. Brown, secretary of Hawaii, W. C. McGonagle, president of the Honolulu Chamber of Commerce, C. N. Arnold, mayor of Honolulu, C. H. Cooke, president of the Hawaiian National Aeronautics Association, and R. E. Wooley, chairman of the Hawaiian Tourist Bureau, all praised Dole in glowing terms and said his offer would be the greatest push for Hawaiian aviation since the dawn of flight. Even in 1927 many Hawaiian businessmen realized the eventual growth of Hawaii would depend greatly on aviation.

Dole appreciated all that was being said, but at the same time he realized some of the dangerous aspects of the race. He was not a flier himself and realized he had no firsthand knowledge of the equipment or preparations necessary for a Pacific flight. Therefore, he wisely turned over the many details of preparation to the National Aeronautics Association and was perfectly willing to cooperate with them. On 28 May Dole telegraphed the Honolulu *Star Bulletin* as follows:

NOW THAT AMPLE ENTRIES FOR HONOLULU FLIGHT SEEM ASSURED WITH EVERY PROSPECT OF SUCCESS I FEEL STRONGLY THE RESPONSIBILITY THAT RESTS DIRECTLY ON COMMITTEE AND INDIRECTLY ON ME THAT EVERY PRECAUTION SHOULD BE TAKEN TO PREVENT OCCURANCE OF ANY SERIOUS MISHAPS. ASSUME COMMITTEE HAS THIS IN HAND AND HESITATE MAKING SUGGESTIONS BUT RESPECTFULLY SUBMIT CONDITIONS FOR CONSIDERATION. ENTRANTS SHOULD HAVE (1) SUFFICIENT FUEL INCLUDING MARGIN OF SAFETY FOR ERRORS (2) SOME MEANS OF SAFELY REMAINING AFLOAT IN CASE OF COMING DOWN ENROUTE (3) AMPLE SUPPLY OF FOOD AND WATER (4) SUFFICIENT FLARES TO INDICATE AT NIGHT. POSSIBLE CONSIDERATION SHOULD ALSO BE GIVEN TO RESTRICTING ROUTE TO STEAMER LANE TO FACILITATE RESCUING IN CASE OF ENGINE FAILURE.

At this stage all thoughts of asking the pilots to drop a letter on any of the islands was dismissed. The committee was naturally against anything that added time or distance to the flight, and Dole was the first to agree.

Now the fringe elements that always accompany any event of importance started to be heard. The Hawaiian Pineapple Company received dozens of letters from men and women saying that, though the writer did not know how to fly, he or she was willing to learn by the date set for the race if someone would provide the plane. Many prominent people in other fields used the race for personal publicity by intimating that they were considering either flying in the race or backing a pilot. It's rather odd that as the race time approached some very good pilots could not find a backer. So the enthusiasm of these prominent people seemed to disappear immediately after their interviews. Numerous hopefuls wrote to James Dole himself asking for financial assistance, apparently not realizing the futility of offering a prize and then providing the backing for someone to win it.

A typical example of such a letter follows:

> Bartlesville, Okla.
> May 27th, 1927

James D. Doyle,
 San Francisco, Calif.
My Dear Mr. Doyle.
  So there is a $35,000 offered for Hops to Hawaii. Please entered my name if ladies can enter. I am no aviator. But I sure can learn and take a chance for the prize. Cant I. I can be ready by the 15th of Aug 1927 or within the next twelve months thereafter. hope to see my name on your list. I remain

> Sincerely yours,
> Rose Anne Schalski
> Box 181
> Bartlesville, Okla.

Thus May 1927 came to a close and the fliers who were seriously interested in entering the contest settled down to obtain backing to purchase and equip an airplane suitable for a sustained flight of 30 or more hours. Though Dole had put a one-year time limit on his offer, it rapidly became apparent that the pilots planning to enter were all hoping to leave as soon as possible. The committee in Honolulu decided that plans should be made to conduct an actual race rather than to leave it to individuals to choose their starting times. It also became apparent that additional safety regulations needed to be established to protect both the fliers and the public.

Though later developments would prove that more stringent rules were needed, the committee did an excellent job with what they had available at the time. It must be remembered they had no previous race experience and little knowledge of what to expect of the entrants. Fortunately, most of the irresponsible people talking of entering would fail to obtain suitable backing. In 1927 a good aircraft engine such as the Wright J–5 sold for 4,850 dollars, and the Curtiss Wright Company had no intention of giving their engines away. Added to that would be 8,000 to 10,000 dollars for an airplane plus operating expenses both before and during the race. This sum represented a small fortune in 1927.

The committee tried hard and labored long hours to minimize the dangers and still to conduct the contest in the true spirit of adventure following the original aims of Dole and the Honolulu *Star Bulletin*. At the end of May 1927 the die was cast. Only time and fate could determine the outcome.

3

BEATING THE GUN

The month of June 1927 was marked by a flurry of preparations, or at least attempts at preparations, for the Pacific Air Race by forty to fifty potential entrants. Interest was building not only in the United States and Hawaii but also in Europe, where some of the more prominent fliers were considering entering. This worldwide interest was most gratifying to Dole because it supported his original feeling that the contest he was sponsoring should truly be international.

A special National Aeronautics Association committee in Honolulu was preparing the rules for controlling the contest and was also preparing aerial navigation charts for the fliers, showing prevailing winds in the Pacific for the month of August. Other charts, showing all available landing sites and prominent landmarks in the islands, were being prepared. As these charts were completed they were forwarded to San Francisco to be placed at the disposal of all contestants. The U.S. Navy's aid was enlisted to supply additional information based on their vast knowledge of the Pacific. Unfortunately many of the fliers planning on entering the contest were neither knowledgeable enough to realize the importance of charts nor were they capable of properly interpreting them. This was not surprising in the year 1927. The Department of Commerce had been working for quite some time on the problems of aerial navigation and was preparing to issue the first airways strip map covering the route from Moline, Illinois, to Kansas City, Missouri. This first of what was eventually to become a complete set of aerial maps covering the entire United States actually went on sale 15 July 1927.

On 22 June the Honolulu *Star Bulletin* reported that Mrs. Martin Jensen, working feverishly to raise a fund of 10,000 dollars to finance her husband's plane, was promoting a special matinee at the States Theatre in Honolulu, with all proceeds to go to the Jensen fund. Ed Mitchell of the Wilbur Melody Players donated the services of his company to Mrs. Jensen for the matinee. Tickets for the 675 seat theater were priced at one dollar each. A good turnout to help finance Hawaii's own flier was anticipated.

Also in the same 22 June issue was an obscure announcement that Lts. Lester J. Maitland and Albert F. Hegenberger of the Army Air Service hoped to fly from California to Hawaii about 15 July. They reportedly expected to take 30 hours and were planning to use a three-engine Fokker C–2 monoplane. Their plane was equipped with the latest in navigational aids, including an early version of directional radio equipment. The report was not completely accurate in that Maitland and Hegenberger had long since passed the stage of hoping to fly to Hawaii and were at Oakland making final preparations for their attempt to span the Pacific. Two other fliers, Charles H. Carter and Ernest L. Smith, were also at Oakland preparing for a Pacific flight. Another obscure article mentioned that Dick Grace, Hollywood stunt pilot, was on his way to Honolulu by ship to prepare for a flight from Hawaii to San Francisco.

By late June some forty fliers had made known their intentions of competing for the Dole prizes. Among them were Claire Vance, prominent San Francisco flier; Ernie Smith, already at Oakland; Paul Redfern, Atlanta, Georgia, pilot who later gained fame flying in South America; Augy Pedlar, a Flint, Michigan, flier; Capt. William Erwin, prominent Dallas, Texas, flier; Prince Serge Mdivani, husband of movie star Pola Negri and a notorious publicity seeker; Rene Fonck, French flier recovering from a recent crash; and Clarence Chamberlain, prominent flier who had just completed an Atlantic flight.

Both the Ryan Aircraft Corporation of San Diego and the Douglas Aircraft Company of Santa Monica released statements that they would back entries, but as it later developed neither did. In fact none of the final entrants used a Ryan or Douglas plane.

Toward the end of June publicity and public interest began to wane. Progress of the fliers in their preparations was not visible to the public. But quite a bit of activity was taking place in the Oakland area for flights not connected with the Pacific Air Race. Ernie Smith, pilot, and Charles H. Carter, navigator, were preparing their original prototype Travel Air Model MA to make the first flight to Hawaii. This airplane had been obtained from the Pacific Air Transport Company and had been modified by P.A.T. personnel. In early June Ernie Smith announced they would hop off for Honolulu as soon as their new Wright J–5 engine was installed and tuned up. Eddie Cooper, chief engine mechanic for Pacific Air Transport, was on a five-day leave of absence from his airline duties. He and a hand-picked crew were working day and night to install and ready the engine. The whole group ate and slept at the airport, working in overlapping shifts in a mad rush to complete the necessary modifications in as short a time as possible. The reason Smith and Carter were so frantic in their preparations was very evident if one looked into the next hanger. There an even larger group, consisting of Lts. Maitland and Hegenberger and an almost endless line of Army Air Service mechanics, were preparing their Fokker C–2 for the same trip. The Army Air Service fliers, with the considerable resources of the Army behind them, had quite an advantage.

Sponsorship by the Army Air Service and the fact they were on active duty eliminated Maitland and Hegenberger from competition in the Pacific Air Race. Their only aim was to be the first to fly across the Pacific, thus promoting the Army Air Service in the eyes of the public. The Service was still smarting from the publicity generated by the flight of the NC–4 across the Atlantic in 1919 and these fliers were determined to "Beat Navy."

Smith and Carter had relatively limited resources at their disposal. Smith, an experienced air-mail pilot, and Carter, a skilled navigator well experienced in seamanship and celestial navigation, were backed by Edmond Moffett, Anthony Parente, and R. E. Wood, all San Francisco businessmen. The present Bank of America also had some interest in the flight, but in 1927 it was known as the Bank of Italy. Bill Broyle was manager of the overall operation. Original plans called for Smith and Carter to fly in late June from Oakland to Hawaii, thus gaining fame for themselves and publicity for their backers. Then they planned to fly back to Oakland in time to compete in the Dole race. Apparently they reasoned if you made a round trip you would know your way better the second time. Ernie Smith felt he could gain fame and fortune surpassing even Lindbergh. From 15 June to 28 June every available member of the ground crew plus Smith and Carter had been steadily working to prepare their plane for takeoff. Oversize fuel tanks had been hastily installed and the new Wright J–5 was ready to go. Sheets of aluminum needed to form the cabin fuel tanks were unobtainable. As a last resort Eddie Cooper fabricated the tanks out of ternplate, a low-grade steel plate used only for engine firewalls. The tanks were heavier than aluminum, but they held the fuel and that's all that counted.

Early on the morning of 28 June with very little fanfare the huge Air Service hanger was opened, and the Fokker C–2 was rolled out. It had already been fueled and loaded with all the necessary supplies. After a short runup of all three engines Maitland and Hegenberger taxied out to the end of the runway, turned into the wind and started their takeoff. Slowly picking up speed they rolled past the assembled Smith and Carter crew. They waved a friendly farewell as they swept by. Ernie Smith yelled a few well-chosen words that he would beat that boxcar to Honolulu, and the entire group returned to their tasks.

About two hours later Smith and Carter hastily scrambled aboard their plane, gave the engine a quick runup and check, and started down the runway hoping to overtake the Army C–2. About five minutes after takeoff part of the navigator's windshield ripped loose, and apparently the altimeter started to stick. Carter insisted on returning to the Oakland Airport to repair the windshield. Seven minutes after takeoff Ernie Smith did a superb job of landing his dangerously overloaded airplane back on the field. He touched down lightly with no damage and taxied back to the hanger. The ground crew immediately started to repair the windshield and recheck the altimeter. But Carter refused to take off again, stating that it was "too late to make observations and anyway the Army plane was too far ahead." He had previously told newsmen that he wanted to start at 10:00 A.M. or 4:00 P.M., yet at 11:15 A.M. he refused to take off again. Possibly the immensity of the Pacific Ocean as seen from the air and the real danger of the whole endeavor had begun to sink in to Carter. Though Ernie Smith was almost sick with anxiety he realized he was helpless without a navigator; finally, admitting he had fallen far behind the Army fliers, he reluctantly called off the flight. While the Army fliers were still in the air many members of the West Coast flying fraternity heard of Smith's plight and a total of five excellent navigators volunteered to make the Honolulu flight with him. They were Henry Linkins, Lt. Cmdr. W. H. Scheetz, Lt. Cmdr. A. H. Eichwoldt, Emory Bronte, and G. J. Petrie.

Meanwhile the Army fliers continued on their lonely way across the Pacific. In some way their Army Fokker was the best available aircraft of the time for an ocean flight attempt. The trimotored plane carried a radio compass, a directional radio receiver, an earth inductor compass, all new and still experimental types of navigational equipment. However shortly after takeoff their entire radio system and all radio aids failed, and they were forced to use the old reliable dead reckoning system of navigation exclusively. The earth inductor compass was still operating, and it was a reliable instrument. They elected to continue on their flight, and after 25 hours and 30 minutes they landed uneventfully at Wheeler Field, Honolulu, to complete the first successful flight across the Pacific.

The fliers were welcomed in true Hawaiian fashion, lavishly wined and dined, and given many awards and tributes. Their big Fokker C–2 was placed on public display for a few weeks and then wheeled into the large Army Air Service hanger at Wheeler Field.

Meanwhile Dick Grace, Hollywood stunt pilot, had left the mainland early in June by Matson Line steamer for Honolulu, with a Waterhouse Cruzair monoplane that he hoped to fly solo from Hawaii to San Francisco.

Beating the Gun

After arriving in Honolulu Grace started to assemble and test his plane. The plane was similar in appearance to the one used by Lindbergh but had only a 36-foot wingspan compared to the 46-foot span of Lindbergh's *Spirit of St. Louis*. Grace's crew, Col. Grant E. Dodge, Lt. Cmdr. Easton D. Koger, and Carl Spangenberger had discovered the propeller had sustained considerable damage during the trip from the mainland and immediately wired for a new one. Grace felt the damage had not been accidental: some of the marks on the propeller appeared to be saw marks. He was convinced that someone was trying to prevent him from completing the flight. Grace, always looking for publicity, voiced his opinion to newsmen, but he never would say whom he suspected. While waiting for delivery of the new propeller a takeoff area was prepared on the famed Barking Sands beach on Kauai near the town of Mana. The plane was altered to allow the leading edge of the wing to hold additional fuel. This was probably the first example of what is now known as a wet wing, in which part of the wing structure is used to hold fuel. This eliminates the extra weight of a separate tank in the wing. A large additional tank was installed in the fuselage extending from the floor to the roof. With these changes Grace had no forward vision at all, and he did not use a periscope as Lindbergh had done. He had one 14-inch diameter porthole on each side of the fuselage in the cockpit area. Through these he could see his landing gear and what was immediately below each wheel.

On 1 July Dick Grace tried to take off but blew a tire. Fortunately a crash was averted. In the next two days he made three more unsuccessful attempts. Finally, down to his last set of tires, Grace elected to take off in the dark shortly before dawn on 4 July, when cooler denser predawn air would provide the lift required for a successful takeoff. After loading his three-week-old wire-haired terrier mascot and her wicker basket in the cabin and stowing a few sandwiches and bottles of water aboard, Dick Grace started for San Francisco. He barely made it off the ground and flew about 50 feet above the waves for many miles before attempting to climb. Less than a half-hour after takeoff he ran into heavy rain and a severe vibration developed in the controls. Grace lost and regained control of the plane a few times before deciding to head back to the Barking Sands. Fighting desperately to maintain control he crash-landed on the beach, striking a tree and breaking both his hands. This was not a new experience for Grace; he had already purposely crashed twenty-four airplanes for various movie studios. His Cruzair plane was demolished, but his dog slept through it. Grace immediately changed her registered name of Kauai Lelani to Dizzy, and as Dizzy she lived on for many years. Grace later stated, "Defective rear controls forced me back to the island of Kauai where my ship and fortune were washed out in a matter of seconds."

Undaunted by his crash Grace released an announcement for the 12 July papers saying he still intended to enter the Pacific Air Race. Then with true Hollywood spirit he further stated that after the Pacific Air Race he would return to San Francisco to prepare to fly nonstop from Seattle to Tokyo. This was in response to the city of Seattle's prize offer of 25,000 dollars for the first flight over that route. The Waterhouse Aircraft Company of Oakland was supposedly building a twin-engine plane for the Tokyo flight. The engines were to be in-line types rather than the popular air-cooled radials.

On 12 July James Dole arrived back at his favorite island and started to actively promote the Pacific Air Race. In an interview immediately after landing in Honolulu, Dole said the Hawaiian Pineapple Company had an attractive proposition to offer commercial aviation in the Hawaiian Islands. He hoped to interest someone on providing air service between Oahu and the pineapple island of Lanai. This would serve the dual purpose of promoting aviation in the Hawaiian Islands and providing rapid transportation for the products of his company.

Meanwhile back in Oakland, Ernie Smith was still determined to be the first civilian to fly across the Pacific. After considerable investigation he accepted Emory Bronte's offer to act as navigator on another attempt to fly from Oakland to Honolulu. Smith still felt that the fame accruing to the first civilian to make the flight would be considerable, and he still had hopes of returning in time to compete in the Pacific Air Race. Naturally the same plane was to be used. The same ground crew again completely checked it out and prepared it for the flight. This time there was no race to beat the Army fliers, in fact they practically had the field to themselves. Both Smith and Bronte had very little sleep in the days preceding the flight. By the time they were ready to leave early on 14 July Smith was a bundle of nerves. As he climbed into the cockpit and prepared to tell his friends goodbye tears came to his eyes. He hurriedly pulled down his goggles to hide his embarrassment, but as he opened the throttle and started down the runway he was having a hard time seeing out over the airplane's nose. But as soon as they were airborne and both of them realized that this was the real thing, they settled down to their jobs.

Shortly after leaving the Farallone Islands behind them they ran into fog and remained in or above it for the next 20 hours. After some 200 miles or about two and half hours their radio failed. Undaunted they decided to continue. Ernie had devised a simple pulley and rope system to be used to pass notes back and forth. On using it the second time it failed. But the engine was performing perfectly and all the instruments were working, so they decided to keep going. Nothing short of an engine failure was going to stop Ernie Smith this time, and when Eddie Cooper said the engine was O.K., it was O.K.

It was almost impossible for them to converse throughout the flight due to the noise of the engine, but they were able to use crude hand signals. They released a few homing pigeons they had brought along, but not a one was ever seen again. They continued to have trouble with their radio, and Bronte tried a few times to repair it. As they approached Hawaii they were unable to tell if their signals were being received. A special radio homing device, built by an Army sergeant, also failed as they approached the islands. Close to the islands the fog had cleared, and the visibility was excellent. When they saw land on the horizon Smith signaled Bronte to try the radio again even though they had no way of knowing if the signals were getting through. The message he sent read: "EVERYTHING GOING FINE. I FEEL AS SAFE AS THE BANK OF ITALY." Naturally the backers were overjoyed to hear from them after 20 hours of silence. The Bank of Italy liked it too.

A short time later they crossed the Hawaiian coastline at a point far from Honolulu, their intended destination. After determining their location, they decided not to take any chances on trying to reach Honolulu. Running low on fuel, with no suitable landing sites in sight, they crash-landed in a tree on the island of Molokai.

Thus ended all phases of Smith's plans for three Pacific crossings. The plane was obviously beyond repair, although both Smith and Bronte climbed down from the tree with only a few scratches and bruises. It was too late to procure another plane even if the backing could be obtained. Nevertheless the flight was considered a success. In 25 hours and 36 minutes they had become the first civilians to fly from the mainland to Hawaii. They stayed at the crash site long enough to salvage the radio and some of the instruments. The remainder was left to the souvenir hunters, and Smith and Bronte were taken to Honolulu for a well-earned rest.

The fame and fortune that Smith anticipated never really materialized, and within just a few days Smith and Bronte left Hawaii on the steamship *President Jefferson*, bound for San Francisco.

4

THE RULES

Now that both the military fliers, Maitland and Hegenberger, and the civilians, Smith and Bronte, had proven that it was possible to successfully fly from the mainland to Hawaii, mixed feelings developed among those planning to enter or to back an entry for the Pacific Air Race. They divided into two groups, those who started to work with more enthusiasm because they were now sure that the prize could be captured and those who felt the glory was gone so there was little reason to risk their money or their lives. Most of those entering the race realized the actual prize money would not cover their expenses. Each expected publicity to provide enough compensation to warrant the risk. Now that a pair of civilians had performed the feat it was becoming evident that the glory would not be worth as much as originally thought. Lindbergh was still basking in his fame. In 1927 the country had been desperately seeking a hero to offset some of the scandals in Washington and the notorious racketeers appearing throughout the nation, and Lindbergh filled the bill. Others would follow and in many cases surpass Lindbergh's feats, but their achievements would all be anticlimatic. He was first and would remain so in the eyes of America. Still, pilots were a hardy breed, and many were ready to fly the Pacific just because it was there.

Regardless of their motives, as the month of July 1927 started to unfold, a group of thirty to forty pilots continued to prepare themselves for what they were sure would be the greatest flight they would ever make.

Early in July the rules were officially released and circulated, and entry blanks were distributed. The official title of the event was North America–Honolulu, Hawaii Trans Pacific Flight. The competition was open to all aviators of Allied nationality holding an F.A.I. certificate as issued by the Fédération Aéronautique Internationale. An entry fee of 100 dollars was established, primarily to separate the talkers from the doers. The committee had been besieged with requests for entry blanks and information, and it was obvious that many of the requesters were not capable of entering. The entry fee was to be sent to the starting committee at the San Francisco Chapter, National Aeronautics Association, at least 10 days prior to the intended takeoff date. As later events unfolded the deadline for entries was changed to midnight 2 August. Starting time was specified as anytime after noon, Pacific time, Friday, 12 August 1927 and for a period of one year thereafter. Starting point could be any place on the North American continent, and the finish point differed depending on the type of aircraft competing. For land planes it was John Rodgers Airport, a new field under construction about four miles west of Honolulu, and for seaplanes, Pearl Harbor, eight miles west of Honolulu. The John Rodgers airport had been named in honor of the first Pacific flier, who had died in a crash in 1926. It was fitting that this airport should be the finish point of the race. The rules further stated that a landing anyplace on the island of Oahu would be accepted. All types of planes were eligible, but the committee wisely required a demonstration of airworthiness and navigability as well as a check of the safety equipment carried before approval would be given. The aircraft had to contain sufficient tankage for fuel and oil for 15 percent more than that calculated to be actually required for the flight. All planes were required to carry a barograph recorder, sealed by the officials, which must not be opened before reaching Hawaii. The recorder was a relatively crude device acting on barometric pressure to provide a record of the altitude flown and thus to prove if the flight had been made nonstop. Where anyone would stop while crossing the Pacific was not known, but the committee wasn't taking any chances. As to safety requirements, the committee stated that suitable lifeboats or floats capable of sustaining the entire crew must be carried. A three-day supply of food and water must be carried along with ten smoke flares or candles. As for radio, the committee recommended that a small semiautomatic code signaling device be carried but did not make it mandatory.

The contest committee consisted of chairman Clarence H. Cooke, president of both the Honolulu Chapter, National Aeronautics Association and the Bank of Hawaii; N.A.A. members Frank O. Boyer, T. A. Cooke, and John H. Kangeter; military representatives Navy Lt. Cmdr. M. B. McComb, commanding officer, Naval Air Station, and Army Capt. L. H. Smith, commander, 19th Pursuit Squadron; and two Honolulu businessmen advisory members, A. W. VanValkenburg and K. B. Barnes.

The starting committee consisted of chairman C. W. Sounders, National Aeronautics Association governor for California, H. E. MacConaughey, vice-president of the Hawaiian Pineapple Company, V. Gephardt, secretary of the N.A.A., and H. Chandler, president of the Los Angeles *Times*. Legal counsel was the firm of Prosser, Anderson and Marx of Honolulu, and depository for the prizes was the Bank of Hawaii in Honolulu.

The rules were brief and to the point. Competitors agreed to be bound by all the rules, to waive any right or action against the N.A.A., committee members, or officials, and to be responsible for any damage he or his crew members might cause. Dole and the committee hoped that responsible, capable fliers would be attracted to the race. At the start no one realized the number of ill-equipped, inexperienced, and incapable people who would try to enter the event.

As time passed and the starting date drew near, a few editorials and articles suggested that the race was foolhardy and dangerous. A few people with foresight realized that the whole enterprise, though worthy in its initial purpose, was the type of undertaking that could easily become a fiasco. If the weather wasn't favorable, or if one or more of the entrants crashed on takeoff, or even worse, while passing over downtown San Francisco, a terrible tragedy could result. The committee was well aware of these possibilities, but they realized there was no way they could eliminate all risks from an overocean race. They arrived at the only sensible solution, to adhere strictly to the published rules and to rely on the entrants' common sense and desire for survival.

In some ways common sense was overruled by the fact that three flights from California to Hawaii had already succeeded, even though one had crash-landed on arrival and one had sailed rather than flown the last few hundred miles. But in spite of a few warnings in newspapers and magazines the momentum of the Pacific Air Race was picking up. All the committee could do was hope for good weather and pray that the contestants would make it safely to Hawaii.

The contest committee had reserved the right, subject to the approval of James Dole, to add to, amend, or omit any of the rules should they deem it advisable. Shortly after the rules were officially released, it became apparent that no contestant would enter a seaplane or flying boat. Seaplanes and flying boats of 1927 vintage were large, cumbersome, and slow. Though well adapted for long range flying, they could not hope to match the speed of the average single-engine land plane. As no flying boat entries were initially received the landing site at Pearl Harbor was eliminated from the rules. It also became apparent that the other landing site, the John Rodgers Airport in Honolulu, would not be completed to the point that it could handle large aircraft or crowds. A suitable substitute was sought. The only one on Oahu Island of sufficient size was the Army Air Service facility at Wheeler Field, a few miles from Honolulu. The Army, already basking in the glory of the Maitland–Hegenberger flight, was most cooperative and offered full use of the field.

The original rules had been formulated to cover a whole year, starting at noon 12 August 1927. Dole never anticipated that a whole group of fliers would be ready on the same day. He originally believed it might take the whole year for anyone to prepare himself and a plane for the flight. It soon became evident that this was not the case. A large number of contestants would be attempting to take off at the same time, and many of them had already indicated they were planning to leave from the Oakland Airport, as it was the only one on the West Coast with a runway sufficiently long to accommodate heavily loaded planes. Most of the trans-Atlantic fliers leaving from Roosevelt Field in New York had either crashed on takeoff or had just barely lifted their overloaded planes over the hills and wires at the edge of the field. This point was not lost on the more knowledgeable Pacific Air Race entrants, and Oakland did have a 7,000-foot runway. The committee envisioned a group of twenty to thirty planes all trying to be first off the ground at the stroke of 12:00 noon on 12 August. They wisely changed the rules to provide a drawing by lot for takeoff positions. Anyone taking off before his turn would be disqualified and ineligible for the prize money. They also designated Oakland as the only acceptable takeoff point.

The rule changes were published, and all concerned agreed it was the only fair and sensible way to run the race. Thus July 1927 slowly passed into history. The start of the race was but two short weeks away, and the final deadline for entries, 2 August, was even closer.

By the morning of 2 August ten entries had been received and accepted. They were:

Art Goebel, Santa Monica, California
Livingston Irving, Oakland, California
Augy Pedlar, Flint, Michigan
Capt. F. Giles, Brisbane, Australia
Charlie Parkhurst, Lomax, Illinois
Norman Goddard, San Diego, California
William Erwin, Dallas, Texas
Arthur Rogers, Los Angeles, California
Jack Frost, San Francisco, California
Benny Griffin, Oklahoma City, Oklahoma

Telegrams and letters were still arriving addressed to F. A. Flynn, chairman of the flight contest committee handling the entries. Among those still planning on depositing their 100 dollars were:

George Covell, San Diego, California
W. R. Garrett, Coronado, California
Harvey Lemcke, Honolulu, Hawaii

Garland Lincoln, San Luis Obispo, California
Cuzon Osborne, Vancouver, British Columbia

A few more stragglers were still hoping to enter if they could beg, borrow, or steal a suitable airplane. These included:

James Giffin, Los Angeles, California
Robert Fowler, San Francisco, California
Marty Jensen, Honolulu, Hawaii
Frank Clark, Hollywood, California

This last group just made it before the midnight deadline, but they made it.

In retrospect, it seems the committee should have established more confining rules concerning the types of aircraft eligible for the race. In 1927 there were two basic schools of thought regarding the type of aircraft best suited for long-distance flying: those who backed single-engine planes and those who insisted a multiengined plane was safer. The single engine backers felt the reliability of the 1927 engines left much to be desired: if fewer engines were used, fewer engines would fail. Surprising as it sounds they were right. A good engine, such as the Wright J–5, could usually be counted on for 40 to 50 hours of continuous running without failing. It follows that the average overocean flight should have a better than even chance of completion if no other trouble was encountered. But a single engine of 1927 was limited to about 200 to 225 horsepower, barely enough to lift a small plane, one or two passengers, and the 400 gallons of fuel necessary for 25 or 30 hours of flight. If additional loads were to be carried, a larger plane with two or more engines was required. Also twice or three times as much fuel was needed, so very little was actually gained. The theoretical added safety factor of an extra engine was nonexistent. A two- or three-engine plane could remain aloft if one engine failed only if it were near the end of the flight and most of the fuel supply was gone. With a full load if one engine failed a crash was inevitable.

Little attention was paid to safety devices such as fuel dumping valves, flotation equipment, or radios. And it was a rare pilot who could afford a plane and a parachute, so very few pilots ever carried one. Most didn't trust them anyway. Of course, the argument that a parachute would be of little use over the ocean also made sense.

Probably the committee should have placed more rigid rules on the load-carrying capability of the aircraft, and insisting on a radio instead of merely recommending it would have been a good idea, but hindsight is always better than foresight. As later events proved, most of the inadequate aircraft either failed to pass the tests or were eliminated by crashes before the start of the race. And ironically, the one plane equipped with practically all known safety devices of the day ended up being lost.

As midnight 2 August approached it still appeared that as many as thirty entrants could be on hand for the 8 August drawing for takeoff positions. Regardless of whether the airplanes were actually capable of crossing the Pacific each pilot thought his was, or he wouldn't have been making his plans.

5

THE LINEUP

As time grew shorter the thirty to forty pilots originally expressing interest in the Pacific Air Race dwindled to about twenty. To start eliminating those without ability, funds, or equipment the contest committee required each contestant to post a 100-dollar entry fee. This narrowed the field considerably. Fees were posted by a total of fifteen pilots. Starting time for the first plane was set at 12:00 noon on 12 August 1927, with each entrant to take off in assigned order at two-minute intervals thereafter until all had gone. Failure to start at the assigned time or a takeoff that had to be aborted for any reason would relegate the unlucky flier to last place in the lineup.

Elapsed time of flight was not a determining factor. The rules stated the first flier reaching Honolulu would be the winner. The earlier one took off the better his chance to finish in first place.

On Monday 8 August, the names of the fifteen pilots were placed in a convenient wastebasket and withdrawn one by one. Takeoff positions were assigned as follows:

1. Benny Griffin, pilot, and Al Henley, navigator, in a Travel Air monoplane, *Oklahoma*
2. Lt. Norman A. Goddard, pilot, and Lt. Kenneth C. Hawkins, navigator, in a Goddard monoplane, *El Encanto*
3. Charlie W. Parkhurst, pilot, and Ralph C. Lowes, navigator, in an Air King biplane, *City of Peoria*
4. John A. "Augy" Pedlar, pilot, and Mildred Doran, passenger, in a Buhl biplane, *Miss Doran*
5. William P. Erwin, pilot, and his wife, navigator, in a modified Swallow monoplane, *Dallas Spirit*

6. Capt. Fred A. Giles, pilot, in a Hess Bluebird biplane, *Detroit Messenger*
7. Livingston G. Irving, pilot, in a Breese monoplane, *Pabco Pacific Flyer*
8. James L. Giffin, pilot, and Ted Lundgren, navigator, in a Fisk International triplane, *Pride of Los Angeles*
9. Art Goebel, pilot, in a Travel Air monoplane, *Woolaroc*, sister ship of the *Oklahoma*
10. Robert Fowler, pilot, without an airplane
11. Martin Jensen, pilot, in a Breese monoplane, *Aloha*
12. Frank Clark, pilot, and Jeff Warren, navigator, in an International biplane, *Miss Hollydale*
13. Lt. George W. D. Covell, pilot, and Lt. Richard Waggener, navigator, in a Tremaine monoplane, *Hummingbird*
14. Capt. Arthur V. Rogers, pilot, in a Bryant monoplane, *Angel of Los Angeles*
15. John W. Frost, pilot, and Gordon Scott, navigator, and Eddie Cooper, flight mechanic, in a Lockheed Vega monoplane, *Golden Eagle*

The committee and James Dole were both pleased and somewhat surprised at the actual number of contestants. But of the fifteen semifinalists some were still destined to fall by the wayside. At the time of the drawing only five contestants could be considered as on site at the Oakland Airport in any condition close to ready to go. They were Benny Griffin, Norm Goddard, Augy Pedlar, Livingston Irving, and Jack Frost. The remaining ten were scattered, as far from Oakland as Dallas and Detroit.

Art Goebel in the *Woolaroc* was making his way across the country somewhere between Wichita and Oakland. Frank Clark, in his *Miss Hollydale*, was in Long Beach, California, awaiting completion of a few details on his plane. Lts. Covell and Waggener were in San Diego with their *Hummingbird*. Marty Jensen, though in Oakland with his plane *Aloha*, was by no means ready to go. Art Rogers, with his *Angel of Los Angeles* was in Los Angeles attempting to complete the necessary alterations to his plane and to tune up the two British Lucifer engines. Charlie Parkhurst, with his *City of Peoria*, was naturally near its namesake in Lomax, Illinois. However he announced he was ready to start and on the day of the drawing he headed west. Bill Erwin was having trouble with his *Dallas Spirit*. He had planned to be in Oakland by 8 August and had attended the formal unveiling and christening of the *Dallas Spirit* at Dallas 6 August. Problems continued, however, and he now planned to leave Dallas on 9 August. The Hess Bluebird and its pilot, Captain Giles, were in Detroit. Though Giles posted the fee of 100 dollars, apparently his problems were insurmountable as he never did arrive in time to start the race. Jim Giffin, Ted Lundgren, and Lawrence Weill, with their plane *Pride of Los Angeles*, were in Los Angeles trying to coax the big triplane to fly. They hoped to leave for Oakland on Thursday 11 August.

It became evident that, even though on Monday, 8 August, fifteen entrants had been assigned a takeoff position, very few of them would be ready to start by noon on Friday, 12 August. The pilots were not alone with their problems. Neither the officials of the National Aeronautics Association nor the Navy and Department of Commerce personnel were ready. Time had been cut a little too short, and most of the pilots and officials had tried a little too hard to accomplish an almost impossible task.

Benny Griffin, a transport-rated pilot of Bartlesville, Oklahoma, had been very interested in the original announcement of the Pacific Air Race on 25 May. After considerable discussion with Al Henley, a fellow Bartlesville resident, they agreed to pool their resources to finance an entry for the race. An Oklahoma City businessman, George Henshaw, agreed to help them. Frank Phillips, president of Phillips Oil Company, hearing that two boys from Bartlesville were planning to enter the Pacific Air Race, offered them all the fuel and oil they would need and the additional cash to cover their operating expenses. Griffin and Henley started shopping for a plane.

Benny Griffin was an experienced pilot who was considered very conservative and careful in his flying habits. This was rare in 1927, when most pilots were anything but conservative. But Griffin never went in for the flashy clothes or the flamboyant mannerisms sported by most pilots. He felt there was a great future in the aviation field, and he planned on growing with the industry. Entering and winning the Dole race could be a stepping stone on his way up the ladder. He hoped the resultant publicity would enable him to become associated with one of the newly formed airlines where he could make good use of his flying ability. After spending considerable time discussing the choice of an airplane with Billy Parker, assistant to Frank Phillips, Griffin and Henley decided they needed a tried and true airplane, preferably one with a large cabin for installation of long-range fuel tanks and enough space for a navigator to work without being too cramped on the long ride across the Pacific. Reliability was far more important to the conservative Griffin than speed.

The Travel Air Company of Wichita, Kansas, had already established a reputation for building airplanes capable of winning races. In fact they were beginning to use the slogan "It takes a Travel Air to beat a Travel Air." Benny Griffin and Al Henley were agreed that one of the newer models, the Travel Air 5000, would be an excellent choice for their purpose. A prototype of the Model 5000, originally sold as a Model M, had already been delivered to Pacific Air Transport, a budding West Coast airline; even then in early June it was being modified by Ernie Smith and Charles Carter for their planned attempt to span the Pacific.

The Travel Air 5000 was one of the best planes in its class. It was originally designed as a high-wing monoplane transport for Pacific Air Transport for mail and passenger service along the West Coast. It carried four passengers and a single pilot in an enclosed cabin together with 50 pounds of baggage and 75 gallons of fuel. The inclusion of the pilot in the forward portion of the cabin area, completely enclosed and protected from the elements, was an innovation for the year 1927. Most of the pilots of that era were still reluctant to be out of direct contact with the wind and the rain. Though flight instrument design was advancing rapidly and many early attempts at actual instrument flying were being conducted, the average pilot still trusted the seat of his pants, the sound of the rigging, and the wind on his face more than the gauges. Instruments were great until you needed them, then you couldn't trust them. This was the general attitude of the 1927 pilot. A few of the more forward-thinking pilots and engineers were convinced that the only way to fly was in an enclosed cockpit. Both Benny Griffin and Al Henley agreed. The Travel Air had been designed with this thought, and this feature alone was a strong determining factor in choosing it for long-distance flying. It had other advantages over many of the aircraft of the day: fully loaded, it could fly at a maximum speed of 123 miles per hour, cruise at 108 miles per hour, and land at 55 miles per hour. Wingspan was 51 feet 7 inches, length was 30 feet 5 inches, and height was 8 feet 9 inches, which made it a rather large airplane for its time. The standard Model 5000 was a typical Travel Air, with "elephant-ear" ailerons, so-called because of the large aerodynamic balance area outboard of the main wing area. The pilot, though enclosed in the cabin, was seated in front and above the passenger cabin. Excellent visibility was afforded by this arrangement, in that the pilot's head was above the upper surface and in front of the leading edge of the wing. Thus he could look in all directions, forward, rearward, and to both sides with comparative ease.

A few minor modifications were made on the basic Model 5000 to improve its performance for the Pacific Air Race. Naturally the passenger cabin area was partially filled with fuel tanks to increase the total fuel load from 75 to 425 gallons. The "elephant-ear" ailerons were replaced with Frieze types, which resulted in less wind resistance but made the controls somewhat harder for the pilot to operate. The pilot's windows were altered slightly, outside steps and hand holds were removed, and the pilot's windshield was lowered, resulting in a further decrease in wind resistance. Most of the original exhaust collector ring was removed from the engine, and short stack exhaust pipes were installed on each cylinder. This resulted in a slight increase in horsepower with a considerable increase in noise.

As the day for the start of the race approached the Travel Air 5000 was completed, painted in standard Travel Air blue and orange colors and christened *Oklahoma*. The name was painted on each side of the fuselage in large white letters, and the registration number NX-911 was painted in black on the wings and tail. The plane was rushed through a few hours of test flying at Wichita by Clarence Clark, test pilot for Travel Air. Griffin flew it during part of the test flying and agreed it was an excellent plane. Then without fanfare Griffin and Henley flew it to Oakland without any mishaps or problems. During the cross-country flight they checked their navigation ability, the fuel and oil consumption, and general flight characteristics of their plane and found everything to their satisfaction. They arrived at Oakland, ready to start, very confident that they had one of the best chances of winning. Only two entries worried them, their sister ship the *Woolaroc* also backed by the Phillips Oil Company and the *Golden Eagle*, built by Lockheed, backed by Hearst, and reported to be the fastest plane of its type in the country. Also Griffin and Henley had a few minor problems keeping the engine cylinder head temperature at acceptable levels. The engine tended to overheat, which in a Wright J-5 could be disastrous. The valves in use in 1927 were not capable of withstanding long periods of high temperature without being "swallowed," that is, dropping into the cylinders. This would result in a forced landing almost immediately. As emergency fields were a long way apart across the Pacific, Griffin and Henley were very concerned about the problem. Henley made many tests trying to maintain an acceptable cylinder head temperature. Ken Boedecker, Wright Aeronautical Company field representative at Oakland, cautioned him about the possibility of burning out a valve before the race even started. Boedecker felt that the Phillips fuel tended to operate somewhat hotter than some of the others and suggested other blends, but Griffin had agreed to use the Phillips fuel and did not consider Boedecker's advice seriously. When the drawing was held on 8 August, Griffin was elated. Certainly the number one starting position was best. With the *Woolaroc* about 18 minutes behind him and the *Golden Eagle* another 12 minutes further back, Griffin and Henley were convinced they would not only be first away from the starting line but first across the finish line in Honolulu.

At the time of the 25 May announcement, Naval Reserve Lt. Norman A. Goddard of San Diego was chief designer, builder, and pilot of a small company, located at 576 Southern Title Building, that was trying to break into the booming aviation business. To date he had built one sport plane. When he saw the announcement for the Pacific Air Race he wondered if his sport plane could be adapted for a long overwater flight. Winning such a race could provide a new airplane company with the publicity needed to start competing with the big producers like Travel Air and Ryan. Goddard announced his intention of entering the race and immediately started adapting his airplane to meet the exacting requirements. It was evident that a large number of modifications would be required. His plane was a high-wing open-cockpit, three-place monoplane, and compared to some of the other entries it was rather small. Wing area was only 283 1/2 square feet, which would prove to be the smallest in the race. For some time Goddard had been using the plane in various races and flying meets on the West Coast, so he was well acquainted with its capabilities. His major problem was to provide enough extra tanks for the required fuel. Goddard approached the problem in a novel fashion. He designed an external belly tank, mounted beneath the cockpit area between the landing gear legs, to carry the major portion of the fuel supply. This kept most of the fuel outside of the cabin and kept the center of gravity low, thus resulting in a very stable airplane in flight. The fuselage was further altered to allow the pilot to be enclosed in a small cockpit immediately ahead of the leading edge of the wing and very close behind the engine. The navigator was seated in the same cockpit in tandem with the pilot and was provided with a set of dual controls. Goddard used what he considered the best engine of the day, the Wright J–5.

Unfortunately, placing the bulk of the fuel outside of the fuselage created a serious hazard, especially in case of an accident during takeoff or landing. The greatest danger would exist during the actual takeoff for the race when the plane would be loaded for the first time to its capacity. If the landing gear failed and the plane skidded on the fuel tank, it was almost certain to become a ball of fire. The landing should be a little safer; no pilot in the race anticipated landing before most of his fuel supply was exhausted. Possibly Goddard incorporated a release system to jettison the belly tank after it was emptied, although there is no record of it. He could then complete the final leg of the race on the fuel in the regular wing tanks. This would eliminate much of the chance of fire or explosion when landing at Honolulu and would decrease the wind resistance considerably, resulting in an increase in speed during the final leg of the flight. Goddard knew the pros and cons of his design, and he felt that the prize was worth the gamble. He was not a flamboyant type of flier like some of the entrants. He had his plane painted a practical silver color. The registration number NX-5074, indicating experimental status as required by the Bureau of Commerce, and the name *El Encanto* were painted in standard black lettering. Mechanically all was in readiness.

As a U.S. Navy Reserve officer, Lt. Goddard was well acquainted with many competent navigators based at the Naval Air Station in San Diego. He talked to one, Lt. Kenneth C. Hawkins, and convinced him to accompany him as navigator. However Lieutenant Hawkins was still on active duty and needed special leave to compete. After some delay and negotiation, Secretary of the Navy Curtis D. Wilbur authorized a special leave to allow Hawkins to join Goddard for the flight.

As Goddard's aircraft factory was located in San Diego, his flight to the Oakland Airport was only about 500 miles and did not provide him with sufficient time to perform long-range fuel consumption tests. He was not too anxious to conduct any unnecessary takeoffs with large fuel loads due to the location of the fuel tank. Upon arrival at Oakland, Goddard met an old acquaintance, Marty Jensen. The meeting perhaps dampened Goddard's enthusiasm, as he was reminded of the last time he had seen Jensen in 1925. At that time he had asked Jensen to check him out in a Curtiss JN-4D "Jenny" and had foolishly bragged that he already had about 3,000 hours flying time. Jensen doubted that and after riding with him refused to solo him. Goddard borrowed another "Jenny" from a friend and promptly cracked it up on takeoff. Obviously he had added to his experience since that time, but Jensen still had doubts about Goddard's ability.

When Goddard drew the number two takeoff position his spirits rose, and he felt he could win. All he had to do was catch up to Benny Griffin in the *Oklahoma* who would take off two minutes ahead of him. He knew his plane was faster than Griffin's, and he felt he had the best navigator in the race. He had confidence in his design and flying ability, in spite of Marty Jensen's opinion, and he convinced himself he would be first in Honolulu.

The third takeoff position was assigned to a real dark horse. Though a representative had submitted the entry fee and attended the drawing, Charlie Parkhurst, pilot, was nowhere to be seen near Oakland. In fact Charlie was still at home in Peoria, Illinois.

Charlie Parkhurst was one of a few transport-rated pilots working for a young aviation enterprise known as National Airways System. The company was officially listed as the "Manufacturers of Air King Airplanes, Lomax, Illinois," but the organizers represented themselves as operating an air service, an airline, flying school, and charter operation. Lomax, Illinois, is a small community on the east bank of the Mississippi River, equidistant from Burlington and Fort Madison, Iowa. Lomax had very little claim to fame, but if the National Airways System became a success Lomax could become a booming community.

S. F. Tannus, president of the company, was intrigued by the Dole offer of 35,000 dollars in prizes. He felt that winning first prize could serve a threefold purpose; provide needed cash, generate favorable publicity to further establish his air service, and produce additional sales for the Air King biplanes, principal product of the National Airways System.

The veteran Burlington, Iowa, barnstormer, Glenn J. Romkey, was the operating manager and part-time test pilot of the organization, assisted by Chet Cummings and Orville Hickman in the design field. Jerome Lederer also served as a consulting engineer, while the actual construction and assembly work was performed by as many as fifty moonlighting local farmers.

Lineup

Charlie Parkhurst was a Peoria, Illinois, pilot who worked part-time for National Airways. He and another Peoria resident, Ralph Lowes, discussed the possibility of entering the Pacific Air Race using a modified Air King biplane. Tannus was delighted with their plan and agreed to supply the airframe. Various citizens of Peoria donated additional money in return for the name *City of Peoria* being emblazoned on the nose of the plane.

The standard Air King was a three-place, open-cockpit, biplane powered by a Curtiss OX-5, 90-horsepower engine. Though somewhat unconventional in appearance, its performance compared favorably with the Swallows, Wacos, and Eaglerocks of the time. Its most important feature was that the lower wing out-spanned the upper by the width of the fuselage. Upper and lower wing panels were interchangeable on the same side. As no actual center section was used in the upper wing, the aircraft had an awkward appearance. However this feature was a big aid to manufacturing and also helped from a maintenance standpoint. "The Air King is the only airplane built to strict N.A.S. standards" was the claim in the National Airways System (N.A.S.) literature.

Parkhurst, Lowes, and Tannus formed a plan to convert a production Air King to use a Wright J-5 engine and modify the fuselage to carry extra fuel and equipment. Lederer strongly advised against this and recommended developing a new design from scratch. However Lederer was involved with other projects and suggested that Tannus hire another engineer, Heraclio Alfaro, of the Martin Company. Alfaro was agreeable and, drawing heavily on his experience with Martin, started to design a new Air King using as many subassemblies as possible from the standard model. After three or four days work in Cleveland, Ohio, Alfaro traveled to Lomax to supervise construction of the Air King racer. On Friday 15 July, Alfaro arrived in Lomax with rolls of sketches and 28 days to build an airplane. The group planned to complete the plane by 5 August and test it during a three-day trip to Oakland. This left 21 days for construction.

All other production was temporarily halted at the National factory, and the construction workers were rotated in shifts around the clock until the airplane was completed. The citizens of Peoria allowed Parkhurst to use the money collected to buy a Wright J-5 engine immediately, as it was needed for test purposes before the airframe would be completed. While construction was going on at a feverish pace, the newly purchased engine was installed in a standard Air King, registered as X-1383, and a series of tests were run. After about five hours of test flying the engine was removed and installed in the Dole Race Air King. Finally on 8 August three days behind schedule, the plane was rolled out of the shop. The entire plane had been painted silver except for a portion around the engine cowling and a stripe on top of the fuselage, both of which were blue. The registration number and other identifying marks were painted black.

Elaborate christening ceremonies had been planned at the Peoria Airport for Sunday, 7 August, but the star of the show failed to make it. About 20,000 Peorians showed up for the festivities, which were to have included Ralph Lowes's seven-year-old daughter, Marilyn, christening the plane, using pineapple juice from Hawaii. Late in the afternoon when it became obvious the plane wouldn't be ready, the ceremony was cancelled, and thousands of well-wishers and financial contributors to the project left the field with mixed feelings about Charlie Parkhurst and Ralph Lowes.

Early the next morning Parkhurst left his home at 4005 South Adams Street in Peoria, picked up Ralph Lowes, and drove to nearby Lomax. The *City of Peoria* was rolled out of the factory; though it glistened in its new paint job, it was far from being ready for a long flight. The earth inductor compass, primary navigation aid, had not been calibrated, and no radio equipment was installed even though they planned to use it. A life raft, donated by the Peoria Advertising and Selling Club, and flares had been installed. Due to the narrow fuselage Parkhurst and Lowes were forced to sit in a slightly staggered position and were still cramped in the small cockpit. At about 10:00 A.M. Parkhurst took off for a brief test flight. He had a few problems and landed in a large clover field near Carman, Illinois. The whole National Airways group converged on the landing site to hear the pilot's report. After a few brief calculations Alfaro announced that 70 gallons of fuel should be added, and then the fliers could start for Oakland, with their first scheduled stop Omaha, Nebraska.

About 2:00 P.M. Parkhurst and Lowes squeezed themselves into the cockpit and started through the clover. Within a few minutes the fuel system started leaking, filling the cockpit with fumes. They were fortunate to be able to land at Lomax. By 7:00 P.M. repairs were completed, and off they went again. This time they became lost as darkness blacked out their "iron compass" and they followed the wrong railroad track. After a few hours they landed in a field near Ottumwa, Iowa, only about 75 miles from their starting point. Early the next morning they started again but damaged the tail skid even though they managed to get into the air. In a few hours they landed at Omaha, Nebraska, having averaged about 93 miles per hour from Ottumwa. After repairing the tail skid and refueling the plane, they headed for Cheyenne, Wyoming. Here their luck changed. It got worse. Parkhurst hit a telephone pole while landing at Cheyenne's municipal airport and ripped off a portion of the lower left wing. Again, repairs were made during the night and on Wednesday 10 August, they headed for Salt Lake City. On this portion of the trip the engine quit over mountainous territory near Rock Springs, Wyoming. Luckily it restarted while Parkhurst was trying to locate flat ground, and they managed to reach Salt Lake City without any further trouble. The next morning they left Salt Lake City, stopped briefly for fuel at Elko and Reno, Nevada, and arrived at Oakland late Thursday afternoon. Judging by the appearance of the Air King when it touched down at Oakland, Parkhurst and Lowes would be lucky to be able to fly it the few miles to the Pacific shore, let alone across the ocean.

S. F. Tannus had left Lomax, Illinois, by train immediately after Parkhurst and Lowes had left by air. He arrived shortly ahead of them and met them at the airport. His telegram to Glenn Romkey back at the National Airways factory has to be the understatement of the year.

SHIP ARRIVED HERE OK STOP NEEDED LOTS OF WORK BEFORE IN CONDITION FOR FLIGHT REGARDS

TANNUS

On 8 August the *Miss Doran*, with pilot John "Augy" Pedlar, was assigned takeoff position number four. The *Miss Doran* and her crew probably received more prerace publicity than all of the other entrants combined. To appreciate this fully we must again return to 25 May when James Dole originally announced plans for the Pacific Air Race.

W. F. "Bill" Malloska, owner of the Lincoln Petroleum Company and operator of the airport at Flint, Michigan, was already planning to sponsor a Pacific flight. He operated a fleet of four, five-passenger airplanes at the Flint airport for general use plus a stunt plane primarily used for advertising purposes. Mildred Doran, a 22-year-old schoolteacher from Flint, had been Malloska's ward for some time. She had always been air-minded, having frequently flown from Flint to Ann Arbor in one of Malloska's planes during her college days at the University of Michigan. After graduation she flew daily from Flint to Caro, Michigan, where she taught a small school.

Early in 1927 Mildred Doran and two of Malloska's pilots, "Augy" Pedlar and "Windy" Sloniger, had conceived the idea of a California to Hawaii flight. Malloska was always interested in any of Mildred Doran's plans, so when she mentioned the proposed flight Malloska thought it was a good idea and told her, "If you want to try it Mildred, I'll provide the plane and all expenses." Mildred Doran was overjoyed and later stated "I was so thrilled I jumped into my car and dashed all over town to tell all my aunts, uncles and friends. Then we began to plan carefully what should be done." True to his promise, Malloska ordered a new Buhl Airsedan plane to be delivered as soon as possible. The day after he placed the order the rest of the country became air-minded—Charles Lindbergh took off for Paris.

It was decided that Mildred Doran would make the flight as a passenger but that only one pilot would be needed. Both Augy and Windy were anxious to be the pilot, each feeling it was his big chance at fame and fortune. The choice was decided by the flip of a coin. Augy won—or lost, depending on your point of view.

When the announcement was made concerning the Pacific Air Race the group was especially thrilled. Now they could not only cross the Pacific as planned but also pick up a sizable prize as well.

Malloska took delivery of his Buhl Airsedan Model CA–5 early in July at the Buhl factory in Maryville, Michigan. This was a standard, five-place, cabin biplane of which eight were built in 1927. The one purchased by Malloska was flown to Lincoln, Nebraska, to be modified by the Standard Airplane Works. There it was altered to carry 400 gallons of fuel instead of the normal 70 to 90 gallons. The lower wing was modified to increase the total wing area slightly from 334 to 350 square feet to carry the heavy load. The Wright J–5 engine supplied the power. A vivid color scheme with red wings and nose, white fuselage, and blue tail was applied, and the plane was appropriately christened *Miss Doran*. The emblem of the Lincoln Petroleum Company was prominently displayed on each side of the cabin and the name *Miss Doran*, was painted on the nose. After some test flying at Lincoln and more at Flint the plane was flown to Oakland by Augy Pedlar with Mildred Doran as a happy passenger. The flight was uneventful and the plane performed well. They arrived about three weeks prior to the start of the race. A few days later Bill Malloska left by ship for Honolulu to be on hand to welcome his friends when they crossed the finish line at Wheeler Field.

After a short time at Oakland Augy Pedlar flew the *Miss Doran* to Long Beach to visit his old friend Earl Dougherty while Mildred Doran saw the sights of San Francisco. While at Long Beach Pedlar met Marty Jensen, who had just arrived from Honolulu and was trying to locate a suitable plane for the race. Pedlar was going to continue flying down the coast to San Diego to have his plane's instruments checked by some friends at the Naval Air Station at North Island. He offered Jensen a ride. Jensen accepted the offer in order to visit the Ryan Company where a plane was reported available.

Of all the entrants in the race the *Miss Doran* should have been the best prepared. The plane was completed some weeks in advance, and plenty of time had been alloted for testing. In their enthusiasm, however, Bill Malloska, Augy Pedlar, and Mildred Doran committed a few errors that would eventually add up to a handicap impossible to overcome. The choice of a plane was good. The Buhl Airsedan was a large, well-engineered, very rugged plane capable, under controlled conditions, of making the flight from Oakland to Hawaii. Unlike some of the other entrants the Buhl was not a sport plane, nor was it a haphazard redesign of an older model.

It was designed as a five-place transport, and its greatest attribute was its load-carrying ability. However, as with any long-distance, overocean flight, fuel would have to be conserved and weight kept to a minimum. The addition of Mildred Doran to the crew imposed the first weight penalty. To make matters worse, special paneling and equipment was added in the cabin to provide her with a private dressing room. Also Augy Pedlar, though he was a competent pilot, was not a skilled navigator and Mildred Doran had no knowledge of the art.

When the day of the drawing dawned, the *Miss Doran* was at the starting line, equipped and tested but the crew was far from ready. Pedlar picked a friend, Marvin A. Lawing of San Diego, as a relief pilot, still not realizing that his primary need would be a competent navigator. But the die was cast, and Doran and Pedlar were basking in the prerace publicity and attention. Almost every edition of the West Coast daily newspapers carried a story about Mildred Doran or Augy Pedlar or both. Possibly a little less publicity and a little more sensible planning would have changed the fate of the *Miss Doran*.

Takeoff number five was assigned to William P. Erwin, a popular and well-known pilot residing in Dallas, Texas. Though Erwin hadn't arrived at Oakland on 8 August to attend the drawing all indications were that he would arrive within a few days.

Long before James Dole made his 25 May announcement, Bill Erwin had been thinking about a Pacific flight. He hoped to be the first to fly from the United States to Hong Kong to claim a 25,000-dollar prize offered by William E. Easterwood of Dallas for the first Dallas to Hong Kong flight. When the Pacific Air Race, with its prize of 25,000 dollars, was announced Erwin included it in his plans and speeded up his preparations in order to meet the required dates.

Erwin had considerable flying experience, held a transport license, and was well acquainted with the danger involved. Before World War I Erwin had grown up in New York City. He enlisted shortly after war was declared and applied for flight duty. He managed to survive the training period and was assigned as an observation pilot in France. He attained the rank of first lieutenant but not before he had more than his share of interesting experiences. He was eventually credited with shooting down eight German aircraft and two probables, giving him a tie with eleven other fliers for the title of thirteenth ranking U.S. ace. He was awarded the Distinguished Flying Cross on 26 May 1919. However a note of irony was involved in his exploits, as he led the other eleven fliers in one respect— he had been shot down five times himself.

For some years after the war Erwin led the life of a typical postwar flier in the Southwest region, flying whenever and wherever the opportunity was offered. With some backing from Dallas friends he purchased a used monoplane. Wingspan was 48 feet, and chord was 7 1/2 feet. Length was 30 1/2 feet, and the wing area was 330 square feet. This particular plane, though nearly always listed as a product of the Swallow Airplane Company of Wichita, Kansas, wasn't a Swallow. It had been built by two former employees of Swallow, and, though many Swallow parts were undoubtedly used, it was actually a very close copy of the standard Swallow monoplane.

Erwin's 20-year-old wife agreed to accompany him and act as navigator. She was looking forward to the trip, little realizing what would be required to navigate over the endless ocean to find a tiny island. As the day for the drawing approached, Erwin, his wife, and his airplane were still in Dallas. But the plane was almost ready, and it seemed that everyone in Dallas was backing Erwin as a Texas entry. The Phillips Oil Company, trying to hedge its bets, offered Erwin free fuel and an agreement to pay him for an endorsement if he won the race. On 6 August, 10,000 people turned out at the Dallas Airport to see the plane officially unveiled and christened the *Dallas Spirit*. After the usual speeches and well-wishes the crowd cheered Erwin and his wife on their way. But the *Dallas Spirit* had a mind of its own, and three more days passed before the mechanics had it purring to Erwin's satisfaction. On 9 August, at 7:18 P.M. they left Dallas on the first leg of their flight to Hong Kong, with short stops planned at Oakland and Honolulu. They had been informed of their assigned takeoff number five. Erwin reasoned that five out of fifteen wasn't too bad. Things looked good at that point, and to all appearances Bill Erwin had just as good a chance as anyone to win Dole's prize.

Takeoff number six was given to Capt. Frederick A. Giles, a British pilot then residing in Detroit. Captain Giles entered a Hess Bluebird biplane under the name *Detroit Messenger*. Few details are available concerning this entry. The airplane was powered by a Wright J–5 engine, the same as almost all the entries. Fuel supply was 500 gallons, and the wing area was 295 square feet. The standard Hess Bluebird of 1927 was a three-place, open-cockpit biplane normally supplied with a Curtiss OX–5, 90-horsepower engine. One model incorporating the same basic airframe, but using a Wright J–5 engine, was offered as a five-place plane for passenger, express, or mail service. According to the Hess Company literature, most of their planes were used for cotton-dusting, photography, stunting, or skywriting. It was an extremely maneuverable airplane with ailerons on all four wing panels and was very well designed and constructed for its time. The Hess Company was located in Wyandotte, Michigan, with executive offices in Detroit.

Apparently Captain Giles purchased a basic model Bluebird with the Wright J–5 engine and the front cockpit containing additional fuel tanks to raise the fuel supply from 30 gallons to 500 gallons. It appears from these sketchy details that Captain Giles had at least a fair chance of successfully completing the race, but as the final day approached he did not show up. He had originally announced his intention to continue his flight westward as far as Wellington, New Zealand, with the Oakland–Honolulu portion being the first step. Apparently the plane was not completed on time or he ran out of funds, as neither he nor his plane reached Oakland in time to compete.

Takeoff position number seven, considered by many to be lucky, was drawn by Maj. Livingston G. Irving, who was present at the drawing, ready and willing to start the race. His plane, a Breese high-wing monoplane, was a tried and true design altered from the original standard five-place commercial version so that it carried 380 gallons of fuel. A total of 15,000 dollars was invested in this plane. It too used a Wright J–5 engine and was capable of a top speed of 110 miles per hour. The wing area was 260 square feet, and takeoff weight was 4,500 pounds.

Major Irving was a hometown boy living at 1240 Bates Road, Oakland, California, the son of S. C. Irving, former mayor of Berkeley. To his friends he was known as Jim. His considerable flying experience had been acquired by flying with the famed Lafayette Escadrille and later transferring to the U.S. Army Air Service. By the close of World War I he was officially listed as an ace. After the war he was employed by the Paraffin Company of Berkeley. When the Pacific Air Race was announced, he convinced his employers to back him, and with their help and some of his own funds he purchased the Breese monoplane for 15,000 dollars. Major Irving was a good pilot holding a current transport license, and he also was a competent navigator. He planned on performing both functions in the race, thus eliminating 150 to 200 pounds of extra weight. With a cruising speed of 100 to 105 miles per hour and a proven range of 3,500 miles he felt he had an excellent chance of winning. He was one of the few pilots in the race to equip his plane with the best of instruments, including an earth inductor compass, radio, kite, rockets, flares, and a rubber life raft.

By 6 August, two days before the actual drawing for positions, Major Irving had his orange and black plane tuned up and ready to go. The name *Pabco Pacific Flyer*, a contraction of the name of his principal backer, the Paraffin Company, was painted on both sides in large white letters, and a small copy of the Lafayette Escadrille insignia was on the nose. The black registration number NX–646 completed the marking. If prior preparations could insure victory, Major Irving was virtually assured of first place. He was capable and ready, and so was his plane.

What was undoubtedly the oddest entry in the race was assigned number eight. This was the Fisk International Tri-plane to be piloted by

Jerry Phillips. When the race was originally announced, Hoot Gibson, one of the most popular of the movie cowboys, was interested in sponsoring an entrant. Gibson was quite active in aviation as a private pilot, and he numbered many of the movie stunt pilots in his list of friends. However he did not have the experience needed to attempt a Pacific flight, nor was he as well versed technically in the aviation field as he thought. He purchased the Fisk International Tri-plane as his entry, or, to be more explicit, a local Long Beach flying service operator saw his chance to unload a white elephant. This was a three-winged, twin-engine plane designed by Fisk of the International Aviation Company of Long Beach, California. The original airplane had two Curtiss OX–5, 90-horsepower engines and had been used for some time in southern California for routine passenger hops. Gibson had the engines replaced with Wright J–5s and installed new, recently developed, special micarta propellors. What had been a passenger cabin was filled with fuel tanks. Between 600 and 700 gallons of fuel would be required to keep the two engines operating for the proposed flight time of 24 hours. When completed the triplane was nothing more than a series of fuel tanks with wings. A single open cockpit behind the wings housed both the pilot and navigator. Visibility was very limited due to the large expanse of wings in front, above, and below the pilot. The plane was also very unstable and in no way suited for long overwater flights. There were reports that Hoot Gibson tried to interest Sir Charles Kingsford-Smith, famous Australian flier, into serving as pilot for his entry. Smith was in the United States at the time trying to obtain backing for one of his long distance flights. He visited Oakland during the preparations for the race but admitted he was not interested in participating in that type of endeavor. He was even less interested in flying the Fisk Tri-plane and made a few public remarks concerning the mentality of people involved in the race and flying the triplane. However, Hoot Gibson was successful in recruiting a crew, which included Jerry Phillips, pilot; Capt. James. L. Giffin, a Long Beach attorney, pilot; Ted Lundgren of Long Beach, navigator; and Lawrence Weill, mechanic and ground crew member. It was never clearly established who was to fly the plane in the race, and as subsequent events eliminated the Fisk Tri-plane from the starting lineup, it probably is of little importance. As of 8 August, at the time of the drawing, considerable work remained to be accomplished to prepare the Fisk for a long flight. It was doubtful if the plane could have been ready by the originally planned starting date. Undoubtedly the crew thought they had a chance to win or they wouldn't have entered, but in retrospect it seems obvious that the Fisk Tri-plane was completely unsuited for the race and the crew was not really capable of the task assigned by owner Hoot Gibson.

  Number nine takeoff position for Art Goebel meant only that he would start 16 minutes behind the leader, Benny Griffin. Goebel and

Griffin were flying almost identical planes and both were using the same Phillips Oil Company fuel, but there the similarity ended.

Art Goebel, of 1161 East 76th Place, Los Angeles, California, 31-years old and unmarried, was probably one of the most experienced fliers in the race, as he had already accumulated more than 1,800 hours flying time and held a transport pilot license. For some years he had been a stunt pilot flying for the various movie studios in and around Los Angeles. Frank Clark, another of the entrants, and Dick Grace, who had originally announced his intention of entering the race, were fellow stunt pilots, and all three had often flown together for the cameras. Art was quite famous in his profession, holding many records for inverted flying, and was considered by the Hollywood stunt men as one of the best. Though he was always ready to tackle any type of flying, he was never foolish or haphazard in his approach to an assignment. Proper planning for the entire flight was a must. This attitude was very evident in his approach to the Pacific Air Race.

When the initial announcement was made Goebel was an independent operator at Clover Field near Santa Monica, California. He immediately rounded up some of his friends to back him as an entry in the race. He risked his own personal fortune of 3,000 dollars, and his close friends added 2,000 dollars more. A Beverly Hills businessman, Cal Chandler, added 4,500 more, and a Los Angeles woman reportedly added 1,500 for a total of 11,000 dollars. This would have been enough to purchase many 1927 airplanes and, in some cases, to equip them for a Pacific flight. But Art was a perfectionist, and he knew his aircraft. He therefore approached Cecil Lippiott, West Coast representative for the Travel Air Company. He was especially interested in their new Model 5000, which appeared to be more than capable of making the flight. On 14 June, Lippiott and Goebel left in Lippiott's Travel Air 4000 for a flight to Wichita, Kansas, to visit the Travel Air Company. After a total of 15 flying hours and an overnight stop at El Paso they landed at Wichita. Here they learned that Walter Beech of the Travel Air Company had already started to build a special version of the Model 5000 for Benny Griffin and Al Henley. After considerable discussion Walter Beech agreed to provide another Model 5000 off the production line, alter it for the Pacific flight similar to the one under construction for Griffin, and deliver it to Goebel by approximately 1 August. However the Travel Air Company wanted more money for their airplanes than Art had managed to scrape together. The entire cost for building, altering, and preparing the plane for the race was calculated at 15,000 to 16,000 dollars. Actually this was a low estimate. Later events would show the entire cost for Goebel's expenses and plane totaled between 19,000 and 19,500 dollars. But at the time Goebel put 5,000 dollars down on a Travel Air 5000 with the remainder due on delivery. Though he lacked about 5,000 dollars in cash, he made up for it in enthusiasm. After signing the contract Goebel and Lippiott left Wichita and flew back to California. The return trip was completed in 16 1/2 hours with an overnight stop at Tucson.

Billy Parker, manager of the Aviation Department of the Phillips Oil Company, had been asked by Frank Phillips to pick from the known entries a potential winner to be sponsored by the Phillips Oil Company. Parker picked Jack Frost in the Lockheed *Golden Eagle* and contacted him. Frost had already agreed to use Standard Oil of California fuel and was being sponsored by the Hearst enterprises. Parker's second choice was Art Goebel, who was, at that point, receptive to any offer of sponsorship. Parker's choice was based on Goebel's reputation as a stunt pilot and the reputation of Walter Beech's Travel Air airplanes. This opinion was probably somewhat biased as Parker was flying a Travel Air 4000 for Phillips and was extremely pleased with the airplane. Parker discussed the deal with Goebel in California, and then he and Goebel flew the Phillips Travel Air back to Bartlesville, Oklahoma, to visit with Frank Phillips. On the way, while Goebel was flying and Parker was dozing, they became lost. This convinced Parker that Goebel either needed navigation training or would have to use a qualified navigator on the big flight.

At Bartlesville Goebel talked to the Phillips officials including Frank Phillips and M. W. Welty, and it was agreed they would provide 4,500 dollars with the stipulation that Phillips fuel would be used and that they would have the privilege of naming the airplane. Phillips's secretary suggested the name *Woolaroc* after the Phillips ranch, and the agreement was signed. The word represented the woods, the lakes, and the rocks, although it was later mistakenly reported in a San Francisco newspaper as being the name of an Indian chief. At a later date Parker admitted he did not know any Breese airplanes had been entered in the race. He considered the Breese a better or at least more reliable and proven plane than the Travel Air. Had he known Marty Jensen would eventually enter a Breese monoplane he would have recommended him to Phillips as his first choice.

Phillips partially financed Goebel's *Woolaroc* and supplied fuel for Griffin's *Oklahoma*. The planes were almost identical, the only noticeable difference being the names in large white letters on the fuselage sides and the registration numbers, NX–911 for *Oklahoma* and NX–869 for *Woolaroc*. Also Goebel added longitudinal angular lines painted on the upper surface of the fuselage and horizontal tail surfaces to enable the navigator to obtain wind drift readings, and his Wright J–5 engine carried the standard long tubular exhaust stacks rather than the short bayonet stacks used by Griffin.

The *Woolaroc* was the last of the two to be completed. Goebel spent quite a bit of time at the Travel Air factory during the last few weeks of

July while the plane was in the final assembly stages. About two weeks before the scheduled start of the race the *Woolaroc* was completed. Clarence Clark, Travel Air test pilot, flew it and pronounced it ready. Billy Parker then flew it and was pleased with its performance. Art Goebel then tried his hand and was most enthusiastic. It was reported that Walter Beech himself decided to fly it before Goebel headed for California. Beech misjudged his approach and landed about ten feet above the airport. The *Woolaroc* stalled in with considerable noise and a big cloud of dust. After a complete inspection it was determined no damage had occurred, and the plane was officially accepted by Goebel. He then flew it across the country without any undue incidents. On the date of the drawing he was still enroute, arriving at Oakland on Tuesday, 9 August. Though he had yet to decide whether to attempt the flight alone or try to locate a good navigator, everything else was in readiness. Goebel knew he had one of the best planes, and he felt he had as much or more experience than most of the contestants. As the starting date approached Goebel was ready, confident, and eager to start.

The number ten position was assigned to Robert Fowler. He was a local boy from San Francisco, and though he had previously posted the 100-dollar entry fee, on the day of the drawing he still had not been able to locate an airplane. On the following day, 9 August, Bob Fowler realized that even if by some miracle he found a plane, he couldn't possibly alter it and equip it in just a few days. Much as he hated to, he withdrew from the race. In just a single day after the drawing, the field had been lowered to fourteen. Odds were starting to improve already.

Marty Jensen, the only pilot in the race from Hawaii, drew starting number eleven. He was another of the contestants who had started planning a Pacific flight before the announcement of the Pacific Air Race. However the planning of a project and the completion can be a long way apart. As events turned out, Jensen just made it to the starting line in the nick of time. On the date of the drawing his plane was still being altered to meet race requirements. The plane, which would later be named *Aloha*, was a Breese high-wing monoplane with a single Wright J–5 engine. From an external appearance it was identical to the *Pabco Pacific Flyer* entered by Livingston Irving. But the fuel tanks and internal fuel plumbing differed greatly. Irving had the benefit of time in reworking his plane, while Jensen was hard pressed to have the *Aloha* ready by the starting date. Wing span was 41 feet with an area of 260 square feet. Overall length was 27 feet. When the airplane was finally ready for the race it carried its two original fuel tanks in the wings and a set of four tanks in the fuselage for a combined total of 405 gallons. A rather complicated fuel transfer system consisting of much tubing and a hand-operated wobble pump was installed, whereby the fuel was pumped from the fuselage tanks up to the wing tanks. From there it flowed by gravity to the engine-driven fuel pump mounted on the accessory section of the engine. Due to the last minute rush of altering the plane, fuel level gauges were eliminated from the system, an oversight that would later cause Jensen considerable anguish.

The *Aloha* was estimated to have a top speed of 110 miles per hour and to cruise at 84 miles per hour. Though slightly slower and more bulky in appearance than some of the other entries, the plane was a well-proven type, one of many built by the Breese Company of San Francisco.

Originally Marty Jensen had intended to cross the Pacific alone. He started making plans at his home in Honolulu while employed by a local flying service, Lewis Hawaiian Tours. He was flying a much-rebuilt, five-place Ryan monoplane between the islands. As with most fliers in 1927, the greatest danger Jensen faced was starvation. His attempt to raise funds among his friends for a projected flight across the Pacific was not greeted with much enthusiasm. However, when James D. Dole announced a prize of 25,000 dollars for the first and 10,000 dollars for the second flier to cross the Pacific from California to Hawaii, interest in helping finance a Hawaiian resident in the race was awakened. Jensen was able to interest a group of local businessmen to sponsor him partially, and by mortgaging his rights to any prize money he might win he was able to obtain enough money to head for California in search of a suitable plane. Meanwhile his wife, Marguerite, usually known as Peg, and some of her friends continued to raise funds to cover the cost of preparations and alterations to the airplane finally selected.

Jensen started with his old friend Earl Dougherty, who was operating a flying service at Long Beach, California. Dougherty knew every pilot and plane on the West Coast for he had been barnstorming and teaching since he left the Army Air Service in 1918. Dougherty did not have a plane suitable for the Pacific crossing, and he suggested that Jensen try the Ryan Company of San Diego that was currently basking in the reflected glory of having built the plane Lindbergh used to cross the Atlantic. Ryan had an M–2 similar to Lindbergh's but it was far from airworthy, and the time necessary to prepare it for a Pacific crossing was not available. A few days before the deadline for posting the entry fee Jensen still had not made a firm deal for an airplane of his own, though he had a few prospects. He invented a fictitious airplane, listing it as a monoplane, 42-foot wingspan with a Wright J–5 engine.

Meanwhile another pilot, Claire K. Vance, intending to enter the race, had contracted with the Breese Company for a plane but ran short of funds. Jensen felt that dependability was the most important quality in the airplane that would win the Pacific Air Race. He knew the Breese airplanes and their reputation. Although they were not the fastest nor the prettiest, they were dependable. He agreed to buy the Breese plane if it could be completed in time. Ten days before the race the wings were bare, the engine was not checked out, and only standard fuel tanks had been installed in the wings.

Jensen was still planning to fly alone, and he had a Navy navigator prepare a flight plan for him. He fully realized that he was not capable of navigation better than basic dead reckoning, but he had confidence in his Navy friend. The course laid out for him was 248° from Oakland for two hours, then 247° for the next two hours, and a continuous change of 1° each two hours, ending with 235° into Wheeler Field in Hawaii after 26 to 28 hours. This did not take into account any wind effect; the strength and direction of the wind would not be known until the actual flight. Jensen took a few hurried lessons on how to determine wind drift and how to correct for it and decided he could find Hawaii.

He originally planned to carry additional gasoline in five-gallon cans and to dump them into the main tank as necessary during the flight. The race committee frowned heavily on the use of fuel cans because of the obvious fire hazard, and they changed the original rules to require that all fuel tanks had to be inspected before takeoff and sealed so that fuel could not be added or removed. This effectively eliminated the use of a series of cans. Jensen voiced his opinion loud and clear that the rules committee was trying to eliminate him from the race. He had planned on using a total of forty-seven fuel cans, pouring each one individually into an internal tank in the fuselage and transferring the fuel to the wing tanks with a hand-operated wobble pump. But the committee stood firm. They further decreed that each aircraft must carry a trained navigator who had passed a basic navigation exam. This rule did not eliminate the pilot from acting as his own navigator, but, even though Jensen held a transport pilot license, he had only basic dead reckoning navigation experience over short distances and he realized he could never pass the test. A few days before the race he started work on altering the interior of his plane to provide four fuselage tanks for an overall 405-gallon capacity. He also inserted an ad in the San Francisco papers for a navigator willing to make the flight.

On the day of the drawing Jensen was far from ready, but if confidence could produce a winner he would be it. His plane was being completed, he had not picked a navigator nor passed his qualifying tests, but he and his crew were working day and night and they all felt sure that Marty Jensen, Honolulu's own, would lead the way to Hawaii.

Another movieland pilot, Frank Clark, of 1949 Tamerind Avenue, Hollywood, California, drew starting position twelve. This entry was backed and managed by C. E. Charlie Babb. Frank Clark had been barnstorming and flying for the movie studios for many years. He was a serious pilot and held a transport pilot license. But movie flying seldom involved great distances. The only navigation required was enough to crash an airplane on an exact spot or hold it steady over a train while the hero or heroine climbed up or down. Clark's choice of an airplane was not the best for crossing the Pacific. He intended to use an International, a product of Long Beach, California. Though it came from the same company that produced the Fisk International Tri-plane, this model was a better than average, standard, two-place, open-cockpit biplane. It is not known how many were built, but probably less than a dozen ever reached flight stage. It was designed as a Model F–17W. Length was 24 feet 6 inches, height was 9 feet 6 inches, and the two wings were of equal span and chord of 35 feet and 5 feet respectively. Total wing area was 325 square feet, and both wings used a USA–27 airfoil. Though the International was reported to have a top speed of 130 miles per hour and a cruising speed of 110 miles per hour, with the alterations required for long-range flying it was undoubtedly much slower. Frank Clark's plane was altered to close in the front cockpit, but the pilot remained in the open rear cockpit. Clark had previously chosen Jeff Warren as his navigator and posted the entry fee. As the date of the drawing arrived, Clark and Warren and their orange and black International with its name, *Miss Hollydale*, prominently displayed on the fuselage, were ready. The name probably represented a compromise based on the home towns of Clark and Warren, Hollywood and Glendale. The entry of Clark and Warren had received very little attention from the press, probably because they were not the typical flashy type of fliers, no undue incidents occurred while preparing their plane, and the plane was a common type seen at most of the 1927 airports. In any case they were the exception to the rule for Pacific Air Race entrants. They were at Oakland and ready.

The number thirteen, considered by most of the contestants to be unlucky, was drawn by Lts. George W. D. Covell and Richard S. Waggener, both officers of the U.S. Navy living in San Diego. On the day of the drawing they were both at their home airport frantically trying to ready their airplane. Waggener was actually a last-minute substitute. Leo P. Pawlikowski had been Covell's original choice as navigator, but fate stepped in and Pawlikowski dropped out because of illness. Lieutenant Waggener, another friend of George Covell's, was asked if he would serve as navigator. He was happy at the chance and pitched in at once to help with the final preparations.

Their plane, a Tremaine monoplane, was the only low-wing type in the race. It was a very plain-looking airplane, square and boxy in shape, with large squared-off wing panels that appeared to be big flat boards. In

1927 a low-wing plane was rather rare, though some had been used quite successfully before, during, and after World War I. However, they tended to be a little less stable than the standard high-wing monoplane or biplane of the period.

Covell and Waggener were sponsored by Fred W. Burgh of Honolulu. He was convinced that, with their Naval Air Service background, Covell and Waggener had an excellent chance of winning. Progress on their plane had been slow, and with the projected start of the race only four days away, they were both working extra hard to be ready. Ahead of them was the flight from San Diego to Oakland, which they hoped to make on 10 August and which would have to serve as a trial of both plane and crew. Then they both faced tests prescribed by the race committee, and their plane had to be inspected and approved. They were cutting their time awfully close.

Drawing number thirteen didn't bother Covell or Waggener though many pilots of the day were superstitious. They had sufficient backing, and their plane was performing as well as could be expected, though it was slow and heavy on the controls when loaded. They had good experience, both flying and navigating, and in two more days they hoped to be in Oakland.

The plane assigned number fourteen in the starting lineup was the second twin-engine plane entered. It was a Bryant monoplane, but, unlike most twin-engine planes, the engines were mounted in tandem with one a tractor and the other a pusher. In other words they were mounted one behind the other in a single nacelle with one pulling and the other pushing. This was not the most efficient method of mounting two engines nor the safest for the crew. The forward engine used a standard tractor-type propeller and was as efficient as any other mounting. However, the rear-mounted engine drove a pusher-type propeller that had to operate in the extremely turbulent airflow resulting from the forward engine. This usually resulted in a drop in efficiency for the rear-mounted engine of about 10 to 15 percent, depending on the distance between the engines and the method of mounting the rear engine. Furthermore, the rear engine almost always ran hotter than the forward one, again due to the restricted airflow. This could further reduce the efficiency. In the Bryant monoplane the pilot and navigator were seated in a cockpit between the two engines. In case of an emergency, they would have to bail out past the rear engine and propeller. If the rear prop was still rotating under these conditions, the bail out could be more dangerous than sticking with the airplane. However no pilot planned to jump out, in fact few even wore parachutes, so this feature was rarely considered. The tail surfaces, consisting of twin rudders, a large horizontal stabilizer, and elevator, were mounted on two long booms extending rearward from the wing. Actually the basic design was very advanced for 1927, though at the time it was considered somewhat freakish.

The Bryant monoplane was also distinguished as the only entrant not using Wright J–5 engines. Instead it used two British Lucifer engines, comparatively small, three-cylinder, radial-type engines, whose greatest claim to fame was their use of sleeve-type valves rather than the conventional poppet types used in the Wrights. The plane itself was not ready for a trans-Pacific flight. Although the pilot, Capt. Arthur V. Rogers, worked day and night, it was not ready on the drawing date for its test flight. If the starting date for the race had not been postponed Captain Rogers would have had to drop out. Nevertheless, on the date of the drawing Captain Rogers was still hoping for a miracle in order to compete. He named his plane *Angel of Los Angeles*, painted on the experimental registration number NX–705, and continued to prepare for the race.

Leland A. Bryant, a Los Angeles architect, was Rogers's sponsor and also the designer and builder of his airplane. Building airplanes was strictly a sideline with Bryant, in fact by today's standards his airplane would be known as a "home built." It was one of a kind, with which both Bryant and Rogers hoped to gain fame and fortune. But on 8 August they had a long way to go, the plane wasn't ready, a navigator hadn't been selected, and the plane was in Los Angeles, 400 miles from the starting point. The outlook for the *Angel of Los Angeles* did not appear bright.

Number fifteen, and last, in the lineup was a Lockheed Vega monoplane named *Golden Eagle*. This plane was considered by all as the fastest entrant in the race. Though scheduled for takeoff 30 minutes behind the *Oklahoma*, most of the those associated with the race felt that the *Golden Eagle* would be the winner. The plane was the prototype of a new design of the recently formed Lockheed Aircraft Company. An earlier Loughead Aircraft Company had been formed immediately after World War I by Alan and Malcolm Loughead, but after completing a few airplanes the company disbanded. Malcolm Loughead formed a new company in Detroit to manufacture hydraulic brakes and changed the name to Lockheed Company because, as he told his associates, he was "tired of being referred to as 'Log Head.'" Later Alan Loughead reorganized the company in December 1926, using the name Lockheed Aircraft Company. Fred Keeler was named president, Alan Loughead, vice-president and general manager, and Ken Jay, secretary and treasurer. They rented a building at Sycamore and Romaine Streets in Hollywood (which is still in use by another company) and started building the first Lockheed Vega. Jack Northrop, who later headed his own aircraft company, was the chief design engineer and was responsible for the name of Vega. The entire cost of the first plane was 17,500 dollars, which included tools and equipment.

Shortly after construction was started the Pacific Air Race was announced. William Randolph Hearst, owner and publisher of the San Francisco *Examiner*, had decided the time had come for the Hearst enterprises to help the budding aircraft industry. He rightly assumed that travel by air, especially across the oceans, would become a big industry. He instructed his son, George, manager of the *Examiner*, that he wanted the newspaper to back a suitable entrant for the Pacific Air Race. A. M. Rochlen, as a personal representative of Hearst, headed the project. He contacted the Ryan Company for a copy of Lindbergh's plane, but delivery could not be made in time. He then asked Professor Merrill of the California Institute of Technology for advice in choosing a plane. Merrill was probably the foremost aeronautical expert on the West Coast, and he immediately recommended the Lockheed Vega. This was enough for Rochlen. After a quick call to Hearst and a short negotiation with Ken Jay of Lockheed, Rochlen handed Jay a check for 12,500 dollars in full payment for Vega Number One. The plane was offered at the bargain price because the Lockheed Company officials were willing to lose more than 5,000 dollars for the opportunity to demonstrate the new plane to the aviation world by winning first prize in the Pacific Air Race.

The Vega was nearing completion at the time the agreement was made with the Hearst enterprises, but there was still time to alter it as necessary for the Pacific Air Race. Hearst had not yet been able to locate a pilot for the race, but Jack Northrop suggested Gordon Scott as navigator. Hearst agreed to hire him for the race, and Northrop offered Scott a temporary position at Lockheed as his assistant. Scott jumped at the chance, left his job of seven years at Douglas Aircraft Company, and joined Lockheed, where he helped design many of the changes incorporated in the Vega for the race.

Hearst also temporarily hired Eddie Cooper as chief mechanic. Cooper, for the second time in his career, took a leave of absence from Pacific Air Transport, but this time it was to serve both as mechanic and as a third crew member in the race.

Meanwhile Hearst was still looking for a pilot. He attempted to hire Edward Bellande, a former U.S. Navy flight instructor, but Bellande turned down the chance. Though he was completely sold on the Lockheed Vega, he felt the flight was too risky based on the rather low reliability of most aircraft engines of the time. Lockheed's original test pilot, Gilbert Budwig, was to test the Vega but shortly before completion of the plane he accepted a position as a government aircraft inspector. Reluctantly he turned down the opportunity to make the first flight in the Vega. Ed Bellande was again contacted and agreed to perform the tests.

The entire staff of twelve Lockheed employees completed the Vega in early July 1927, and on 4 July the first flight was made from a hayfield near Englewood, California. This hayfield later became the southwest corner of the present Los Angeles International Airport. The first flight lasted an hour, and Ed Bellande was extremely pleased with the airplane's performance. Meanwhile Hearst and Rochlen had been introduced to Jack Frost by Ken Jay of Lockheed. Frost had been a student of Jay's during the war; though he had not flown for about five years, he had been an excellent pilot. His manner and appearance impressed Hearst and Rochlen, and they offered him a job as pilot.

Early in July Ed Bellande flew the Vega to the Hearst estate at San Simeon near Los Angeles where Mrs. George Hearst officially christened the plane *Golden Eagle*. It was then flown to Oakland and turned over to Jack Frost.

The Vega was painted bright orange with red trim and carried the Lockheed star trademark on the vertical fin, the Lockheed name and registration number 2788 on the rudder, and the name *Golden Eagle* in small letters on the side of the fuselage.

The Vega was undoubtedly the best overall design entered in the race. It was a high-wing monoplane designed to carry four to six passengers plus pilot. It was 27 feet 6 inches long, had a 41-foot wingspan, and was 8 feet 4 1/2 inches high. The pilot sat in an open cockpit at the leading edge of the wing, well protected by a large wind screen. A Wright J–5 engine, uncowled, with short exhaust stacks was mounted on the streamlined nose. Top speed was computed at 135 miles per hour, cruising speed at 118 miles per hour, and landing speed at 49 miles per hour. Fuel capacity was 350 gallons in three 50-gallon wing tanks and two 100-gallon fuselage tanks. Many special features were designed into the plane to improve the performance and to increase the safety factor in case of an emergency landing at sea. Landing gear that could be released in case of a water landing, carbon dioxide operated flotation bags—in the wing tips, beneath the pilot's seat, and at the rear of the fuselage—and a special cork packing in the base of the fuselage would all help the plane remain afloat if necessary. In addition, doors and windows were lined with special sealant to keep out the sea. It was estimated that, if a soft landing could be made at sea, the *Golden Eagle* could remain afloat 30 days. To offer further protection a rubber life raft equipped with paddles, food, water, large sail, removable compass, flares, and smoke bombs was carried. Alterations were made to the fuselage to provide a special navigation hatch at the trailing edge of the wing, and a separate instrument panel with the latest navigational instruments was provided for Gordon Scott. The plane was assigned a new registration number, NX–913. Apparently a few of the entrants were registered shortly before the race as numbers NX–911, 913, and 914 were all used.

Jack Frost spent most of July checking out the *Golden Eagle* and setting many intercity records such as Los Angeles to Oakland in 3 hours, 5 minutes. Eddie Cooper and Gordon Scott accompanied Frost on many of these flights. Scott, born in Santa Monica and raised on the West Coast, had worked for seven years as an engineer for Douglas Aircraft. He was also known as an expert navigator. Eddie Cooper was born in England where at the early age of fourteen he started to work in an aircraft factory. A few years later he came to the United States, where he became an excellent engine mechanic.

Jack Frost also had considerable experience. Born in Chicago in 1898, he enlisted in the Army Air Service in 1917 and became an instructor in aeronautics and gunnery. He was on his way to France when the Armistice was signed. He later became known as New York City's first aerial policeman. At one time he served as assistant postmaster of the United States. Later he developed a successful Wall Street bond business, which he left to enter the Pacific Air Race. Frost claimed 2,500 hours of flight time, which was probably somewhat of an exaggeration, but he was rusty after a five-year layoff from flying. On one of his first flights in the *Golden Eagle* Eddie Cooper, while standing behind Frost in the cabin, had to reach forward to the control column to demonstrate some of the finer points of landing the sensitive Vega. Frost wasn't used to what was, for its day, a high-performance airplane, and this was the real reason he continued to make many practice flights in the *Golden Eagle* in the weeks before the race.

The team of Scott, Cooper, and Frost was considered by many to be the most experienced team in the race, and there was no doubt they were flying the best-performing and best-equipped plane. What many of the contestants didn't know was that about a week before the drawing date the team plus Jack Northrop had flown the *Golden Eagle* to the San Diego Naval Station at North Island to have the instruments checked. Part of the airport at the Naval Air Station had once been a golf course. On takeoff they unfortunately hit a hidden sand trap, damaging the landing gear and fuselage. Temporary repairs were made by Army and Navy personnel to allow them to return to Los Angeles. A few days and nights of activity and the *Golden Eagle* was again ready to go. But it bore the obvious scars of the incident up to the day of the race.

Hearst was also financing construction of a Lockheed low-wing seaplane for a flight from California to Australia. The crew of the *Golden Eagle* hoped to win the Dole prize, fly back to California, and then fly the newer seaplane to Australia.

On the day of the drawing for takeoff positions the *Golden Eagle* was ready. Though it was assigned last place in the starting lineup, it appeared to those in the know that it would be in first place in Honolulu.

6

THE MAD SCRAMBLE

After the list of entrants was finalized the pace of preparations was stepped up to meet the starting date of Friday, 12 August.

On Tuesday Bob Fowler was still a pilot without an airplane. At this late date he had little choice—he withdrew his application. Frank Clark arrived at Oakland in his plane, the *Miss Hollydale*. The plane appeared to be in excellent shape, and Clark appeared to be happy and ready to start on his great adventure. It came as quite a surprise to all when Frank Clark announced that he might withdraw. He gave no reason, but possibly he realized the enormous gamble that was involved and was having second thoughts. In any case he made no attempt to take the required tests and continued to keep everyone guessing as to his final decision. A later newspaper article stated that Clark had determined the trip was too dangerous for the type of aircraft he was flying.

Art Goebel arrived in his *Woolaroc*, greeted his many California friends, and began his campaign to convince all listeners that he would surely win. He had been accompanied on his cross-country trip by Billy Parker in his trusty Travel Air 4000. Upon arrival Parker insisted that Goebel visit the Matson Steamship Line and spend some time with some of their officers to learn at least the rudiments of navigation. After spending much time with Goebel and having flown with him a few times, Parker was beginning to doubt his own ability to pick a winner. He consoled himself, however, that Phillips had also provided some backing for Benny Griffin in the *Oklahoma* and was supplying fuel for Bill Erwin in the *Dallas Spirit*. It appeared that Phillips had about a one-in-three chance of being associated with a winner. Parker was also beginning to realize that Goebel, though extremely skillful as a pilot, was not the most popular kid on the block with the West Coast flying fraternity. Some were vocal in their wishes that Goebel wouldn't even get off the ground.

The race committee announced that they were ready to start checking out the aircraft, pilots, and navigators and that they would conduct all three tests simultaneously. Navy Lt. Ben Wyatt, a respected navigation expert, had been selected to handle the navigator testing. The Navy was especially interested in holding down the costs of search and rescue missions for downed fliers. So they agreed to grant Ben Wyatt all the time and assistance he needed to handle the testing. Walter Parkin and Bill Breingan, skilled mechanics, were picked to inspect the aircraft and the food and safety supplies. Art Starbuck, a Department of Commerce pilot, was to fly each plane through a set series of tests to determine cruising speeds and fuel-consumption rates. Each plane was completely inspected for proper equipment including floats or life belts, three-day supply of food and water, emergency signaling equipment, and sufficient gasoline and oil capacity. The planes were then flown at a standard throttle setting to establish a cruising speed, and a fuel-consumption rate was determined.

Actually the test flights proved little. Due to the danger involved, the planes were not loaded even close to their actual capacity but were flown with approximately 50 percent of their normal load. This meant that any calculated range or fuel-consumption rate was at best only an educated guess. But the tests would eliminate planes obviously incapable of flying the required distance nonstop and eliminate pilots and navigators who didn't have enough sense to realize the hazards involved. According to the rules, the total fuel and oil capacity had to be 15 percent in excess of that required to fly 2,400 miles at normal cruising speed. The pilot had to demonstrate his ability to handle his own plane in both normal and abnormal attitudes and flight conditions, and each navigator had to prove his familiarity with dead reckoning and to have at least a token knowledge of celestial navigation. A few of the pilots were planning to act as their own navigators, which was permissible if they could demonstrate sufficient skill to pass both tests. The *Golden Eagle* and *Pabco Pacific Flyer* were the first planes submitted for testing. It was beginning to look like a race might shape up after all.

Wednesday, 10 August, there were eight entries at the Oakland Airport. Four of these, the *Oklahoma*, *El Encanto*, *Pabco Pacific Flyer*, and *Golden Eagle*, could be considered ready to fly. Three others, the *Miss Doran*, *Aloha*, and *Woolaroc* were in various stages of assembly, repair, or testing. The eighth, *Miss Hollydale*, though ready and able, had already, at least verbally, been withdrawn by Frank Clark. Early in the day the *Golden Eagle* became the first plane to officially qualify, followed closely by the *Pabco Pacific Flyer*. Tests for pilots were started and Jack Frost and Livingston Irving passed easily. Marty Jensen announced his choice of a navigator, Paul Schluter, a West Coast ship's captain with considerable experience. Schluter had never flown, but he was looking forward to the race like a schoolboy. Bill

Erwin was still enroute from Dallas, Texas, and was in for a surprise. His wife, who had originally told the press she would fly with her husband as a navigator, was being asked by the committee to step down as a crew member, because of her young age of twenty. Late in the afternoon a report spread throughout the Oakland Airport that the Tremaine *Hummingbird* had crashed in San Diego. For a short time hope was held that the pilot, George Covell, and the navigator, Dick Waggener, might have survived, but it was not to be. The two had taken off near noon from the North Island Naval Station while the usual light San Diego haze covered the bay. Heading south over the ocean to take advantage of the prevailing onshore breeze and lack of obstructions they started to climb. Their progress was watched by Mrs. Covell, Dick Waggener's fianće, Virginia Powell, and a small group of well-wishers. As the *Hummingbird* headed out over the ocean Covell and Waggener could see the magnificent Del Coronado Hotel out the left side and Point Loma out the right. Their view directly ahead was restricted due to the design of their plane. They waved to the many swimmers in the surf and slowly climbed up into the hazy sky. After a few minutes they started a shallow turn to the right to fly back over the Naval Air Station toward Oakland, 600 miles north. Whether the wind shifted or whether they miscalculated their rate of climb or speed will never be known, but they headed directly west toward the barren side of Point Loma, the familiar landmark for all San Diego fliers and sailors. The small crowd, watching from the shore, had been joined by the full crew of the *Golden Eagle*. They had just arrived from Oakland to have a last check made on their instruments. The group, Jack Frost, Gordon Scott, Eddie Cooper, and Jack Northrop, started to yell and the whole crowd joined in, "Pull up—pull up," but it was no use. Helplessly they watched, unable to believe what they were seeing. Apparently neither Covell nor Waggener could see over the nose of the aircraft. Maybe some mishap occurred in the cabin that caught their attention, perhaps the controls jammed for some unexplained reason. In any case the Tremaine *Hummingbird*, heavily loaded with the fliers equipment and fuel for the flight to Oakland, flew straight into the side of Point Loma and burst into flames. Both fliers died instantly. Ironically, George Covell had drawn number thirteen for takeoff.

News of the crash saddened all participants and their crews at Oakland, but pilots in 1927 were no strangers to death. Each faced it, accepted it, and convinced himself that it only happened to the other guy. Each crew continued its preparations, a little sadder but a little more determined not to meet the same fate.

Thursday, 11 August, Bill Erwin arrived in the *Dallas Spirit*. He was met by the unexpected news that the race committee would not allow his young wife to serve as his navigator. After some discussion Erwin announced that he would fly alone, acting as both pilot and navigator.

Erwin had to contend with some other problems. His plane was never built to carry the excess weight required for the Pacific flight. The landing gear legs and axles were beginning to show evidence of the strain and to bend dangerously. But Erwin was reluctant to take the time for repairs with the start of the race so close. He decided to take a chance, as he should have to take off only once with a full load and didn't plan on landing again until the fuel was almost gone.

The *City of Peoria*, after an extremely hectic trip across the country, finally arrived. Charlie Parkhurst, pilot, and Ralph Lowes, navigator, were apparently not pleased with the plane's performance and rightly so. They had suffered a forced landing due to fuel leaks, damage during takeoff to the tail skid, damage to a lower wing by taxying into a telephone pole, and a slow cruising speed varying from about 60 to 93 miles per hours. Once the engine quit while they were in the air, but Parkhurst had been able to restart it before reaching the ground. Owner S. F. Tannus met the weary fliers, and they discussed the situation. Both Parkhurst and Lowes were not in the best of moods and were very dubious about continuing the flight, but they did agree to go ahead with the pilot and navigator tests. In the next few days Tannus became so infuriated with Parkhurst's and Lowes's attitudes that he apparently discharged them. When it was pointed out to him that many people in Peoria had contributed money to the project because Charlie Parkhurst was the pilot, he reacted by having the name *City of Peoria* painted over on the cowling and looking for a new crew. Tannus had been accompanied by his business manager, Edward Lagron, and the word quickly spread that if Parkhurst wouldn't fly the plane Lagron would. Tannus had started to calm down after his initial outburst and decided not to paint over the crew members' names on the sides of the plane, still hoping he could convince them to make the trip. This accounts for the various photos of the *City of Peoria*, some with the name and some without but almost all with the crewmen's names still on the sides. Evidently Parkhurst and Lowes wanted equal billing because on the right side the lettering read:

C. W. PARKHURST, PILOT
R. C. LOWES JR., NAVIGATOR

On the left side Lowes got top billing.

Late in the afternoon all activity on the ground halted as the Fisk Tri-plane appeared over the bay on its way to land at the Oakland Airport. Jim Giffin, Ted Lundgren, and Lawrence Weill were about to arrive after flying their big triplane from Los Angeles. For most of the spectators this was an unforgettable sight. If you didn't see the Fisk you would not believe it. The Fisk didn't even look like an airplane. With three sets of wing panels and two engines mounted on the lower wing it appeared to be some ancient flying machine dreamed up by Jules Verne. Though hard to believe, it was flying. Whether it could stay in the air long enough to cross the Pacific was debatable, but today it was flying. Practically everyone at the airport was watching as Giffin, Lundgren, and Weill started their approach. Throttling back as they entered the traffic pattern they entered the base leg out over the bay and started the final left turn to line up with the runway at about 200 feet of altitude. At that moment a small plane, many of which were always in the air, turned sharply in front of the hugh triplane. To avoid a collision Jim Giffin advanced both throttles wide open, intending to circle the field before landing. The right engine obediently roared—the left coughed and died. Already in a left bank the big triplane settled slowly, almost grotesquely, the left wing sliding down toward the mud and shallow water at the end of the runway. With a huge splash the plane made a three-point landing: wing, wheel, and nose. Before the crowd could reach the crash scene all three of the occupants had crawled out, bruised, scratched, and soaking wet but fortunately not seriously hurt. The biggest injury was to their pride. The triplane was not as lucky and appeared to be a total loss, or almost. Marty Jensen, working on his *Aloha*, had been having another problem. His fuel pump was erratic, and he had exhausted all local sources for a replacement pump. As soon as he saw the crew of the triplane emerge he headed toward them, not to express his regrets or sympathy, but to dicker with them for a fuel pump from one of their submerged engines. They agreed to let him use one of the pumps. Though Jim Giffin and his crew were out, at least part of their aircraft would still be in the race in Marty Jensen's *Aloha*.

With only two planes and crews approved and the starting time less than 24 hours away, the race committee called a special meeting of the pilots and discussed delaying the starting date for a few days. They pointed out that a last minute rush in preparations had probably already contributed to the two crashes and that there wasn't sufficient time left to completely check all the remaining entrants even if they could all be made ready. A few of the entrants were actually ready to go, and no one could blame them if they insisted on sticking to the original rules as to a starting date. But none of them wanted to win a race that way nor did they want to be the cause of a flier's taking off unprepared and being lost at sea, so the entrants voted among themselves and announced they would agree to a delay. It was decided to allow four additional days of preparation. Cables were sent to James Dole and the committees in Hawaii to tell them of the new starting date. Early in the evening the decision was announced and the new starting date of 16 August was made official. It was stressed that if any pilot left before the new date the race committee would disqualify him. Frank Clark did not agree with the decision, and, though he had previously announced his intention to withdraw from the race, he now let it be known that he and Charlie Babb, his financial backer, would attempt to beat the world's endurance record in his International *Miss Hollydale*. The other contestants smelled a rat.

Clarence Young, in order to calm the remaining entrants, announced he would revoke the license of any pilot taking off before 16 August or without the official sanction of Ben Wyatt. The committee also decided the new order of takeoff would follow the original order unless the plane had not been ready to take the qualification tests on 12 August. Qualifiers after that would start in order of qualification. This allowed the contestants who were originally ready before the final qualifying date at least a few minutes lead over the late qualifiers. It was further agreed that if a plane did not take off at its prescribed time it was to be rescheduled at the end of the starting lineup.

Friday, 12 August. Some of the fliers had tried to obtain insurance for their flight. Also many people were attempting to place bets on individual entrants. Early on Friday, Charles Barnholt, San Francisco representative for Lloyds of London, announced that he would not handle any insurance on the race, neither would he quote odds for or against any pilot or plane.

Friday was relatively quiet. Most of the fliers appreciated the four extra days delay and spent the day continuing to prepare their planes. Two contestants still hadn't arrived. Captain Giles was still in Detroit with his Hess Bluebird, and Arthur Rogers with his Bryant monoplane was reported ready to leave Los Angeles. A brief race program listing eleven remaining starters, their planes, and crew members was released to the press and placed on sale to the public.

Marty Jensen decided this was a good time to take Paul Schluter, his navigator, for his first airplane ride. Jensen treated him to a series of rolls, loops, and spins. Schluter, though not overly pleased, came through it remarkably well and still agreed to act as navigator, even after being told he could not expect any pay. Jensen had mortgaged all possible winnings to help finance his plane, and his wife was still trying to raise additional funds. Schluter said "I will go for the glory." Jensen was still planning to equip his plane with a radio and was assigned call letters KGGJ.

At this point in the late afternoon misfortune again intervened. Art Rogers decided he was ready to leave Vail Field in Los Angeles for the flight to Oakland. Lt. Vilas Knope, a Navy navigator, had just obtained leave and hoped to reach Oakland in time to talk his friend Augy Pedlar into adding him to the crew of the *Miss Doran*. He asked Rogers for a ride to Oakland, but Art refused. Knope was not very happy at that moment, facing a long train ride. After a final check, Rogers told his wife, Mary Louise, Vilas Knope, and various other friends goodbye and climbed into his plane. Running both engines until he was satisfied, he started down the runway. From all reports he took off normally and started to climb slowly but not slow enough. The heavily loaded twin-engine plane stalled as it reached the edge of the field. Rogers tried to bail out, as he was one of the few 1927 pilots who believed in parachutes, but he was too low and too slow. His chute only partially opened and he died the moment he hit the ground. With four days to go the entry list was down to ten.

Saturday, 13 August. Again a sense of gloom was felt at the Oakland Airport when the news of Rogers's death reached the field. That evening in many of the Oakland speakeasys the lines sung so often by pilots during the war were sung again:

> But stand to your glasses steady
> We drink to our comrades eyes.
> Quaff a cup to the dead already,
> And hurrah for the next that dies.

But most of the contestants still had much to do before they could say they were ready, and they could spare no more than a few passing thoughts as to what happened to Rogers. Most of them blamed the British Lucifer engines, assuming that they were not as reliable as their own Wright J–5s.

The starting committee announced that the final deadline for all qualifications would be 10:00 A.M. Monday, 15 August. The *Oklahoma, El Encanto,* and *Miss Doran* were all approved as numbers three, four, and five. Augy Pedlar announced that M. A. Lawing, his original choice for navigator, had failed the test and was replaced by Lt. Vilas Knope, who had just arrived by train from Los Angeles. Knope, though shaken by his near miss with death in Los Angeles, was still anxious to go on the great adventure. He immediately applied for the navigator test and had no trouble passing it. As a qualified Navy navigator he should be a big help to Augy Pedlar and Mildred Doran.

Bill Erwin made good use of the delay in the starting date by removing the landing gear from his *Dallas Spirit* and having the main tubing hardened and heat-treated at a local machine shop. This would solve his problem of a sagging landing gear.

The *City of Peoria* was checked out by the committee and passed, though doubts as to its ability to reach Hawaii were expressed by some. Ralph Lowes passed his navigation test with flying colors. S. F. Tannus and Charlie Parkhurst were still not on the best of terms, but at least they hadn't come to blows.

Bill Erwin agreed with the committee's request to replace his wife as navigator and also changed his mind about flying alone. He named as navigator Alvin Eichwoldt, who was immediately approved.

Late in the afternoon a flurry of activity was noted around Frank Clark's *Miss Hollydale*. The Standard Oil of California truck arrived and apparently filled the plane's tanks to their limit of 400 gallons. Speculation immediately ran riot throughout the field as to Clark's intentions. It was the day after the original 12 August starting date, and some of the pilots were still not convinced that the first to arrive in Hawaii would not be accepted by James Dole as a winner. Clark had a reputation for being a devil-may-care type of pilot so he could have anything in mind. He and Charlie Babb climbed aboard their plane shortly before 5:00 P.M., brushed off all questions concerning their destination, and prepared to take off. Just before starting the engine they were questioned again by reporters. They still gave out vague answers about beating the endurance record. A few minutes after five they said good-bye, took off, and headed west through the Golden Gate toward Hawaii.

Now the remaining pilots were upset—afraid that Clark was headed for Honolulu and fearing if he made it he could legally claim the prize of 25,000 dollars according to Dole's original rules. Ben Wyatt, busy with his check-out duties, tried to calm them down. He reminded them again of the revised rules that disqualified any pilot taking off in advance. A short while later word was received that Clark and Babb had landed at Clover Field in Santa Monica, where they had a good laugh at the expense of the other contestants.

Sunday, 14 August. This was Marty Jensen's day. By now he was being referred to as the "Aloha Kid." After an extremely hectic week of working almost continuously on his Breese monoplane he felt he needed some relaxation as well as publicity. He persuaded Ruby Smith, Miss Oakland in the 1925 Miss America contest, to christen his plane with a bottle of water "from the Pacific Ocean near the Hawaiian Islands." His only reaction was a broad grin when a reporter suggested he had seen the water come out of the faucet in his hotel room that morning. Hired Hawaiian singers and hula dancers performed for the press, and a Hawaiian lei was painted around the nose of the plane. The official seal of the territory of Hawaii was painted on the side of the plane's cabin, and Jensen, together with his navigator, Schluter, were almost ready to go. Sunday passed slowly and quietly. Most of the pilots made a few test flights, adjusting their engines endlessly and spent the day at the airport discussing their chances of reaching Hawaii. The press, as usual, was present, and a few thousand visitors talked to the fliers and looked over the airplanes. The crowds were beginning to show more interest as the starting date approached and the press increased their coverage. Mildred Doran continued to receive the most attention and appeared to be enjoying it to the fullest.

Eddie Cooper, working on the *Golden Eagle*, was pleasantly surprised when his wife arrived carrying their baby daughter. He proudly showed them the *Golden Eagle* and introduced them to the other crew members. Up to this time Ken Jay and Jack Northrop hadn't realized that Cooper was a new father. This put a new light on their plans. Both Jay and Northrup agreed that Cooper should not be allowed to accompany Jack Frost and Gordon Scott to Hawaii, just in case something went wrong. Jack Northrop told Cooper that he wouldn't allow him to fly in the race, using the excuse that his additional weight would impose too great a handicap on the plane. Besides, the best engine mechanic in the world probably couldn't help much if trouble developed in the air. Cooper was disgusted: he pleaded, he threatened, but he finally resigned himself and went back to checking out the engine.

Monday, 15 August. Bill Erwin qualified early in the morning as the sixth pilot, followed shortly by Marty Jensen as the seventh. Art Goebel had some trouble with his landing gear during a test flight, and for a while it appeared that he might end up in a crash-landing. Being an accomplished stunt pilot, Art leaned far out of the plane, hung down over the landing gear, and managed to make some temporary repairs so that he could safely land the plane. After landing he repaired the gear and then calmly checked out as pilot number eight.

There were now nine racing airplanes on the field. There still seemed to be some doubt about the *City of Peoria*, and the Hess Bluebird had not yet arrived from Detroit. Charlie Parkhurst qualified as both pilot and navigator for the *City of Peoria* even though Ralph Lowes had previously qualified as navigator. Marty Jensen took his plane up for an hour and a half to practice flying and to give Paul Schluter some much needed experience.

It was reported that six planes were carrying radios. Jack Frost had both a transmitter and receiver and was using call letters KWS. Benny Griffin was using a transmitter operating on 592 meters with the call letters KOE. Norm Goddard had a transmitter on 600 meters using call letters KOK. Livingston Irving was to transmit on 88.1 meters with call letters KGGA. Art Goebel would operate on 608 meters with call letters KGGI. Marty Jensen was still expecting to use a radio but had not received the special set promised him before he left Hawaii.

By late afternoon or early evening all activity came to a halt at the Oakland Airport. If the plane crews were not ready by this time they never would be. There still seemed to be some question whether the *City of Peoria* would be allowed to take off, based on its fuel capacity and rate of consumption. Both Tannus and Parkhurst were still visibly agitated and seemed to differ on whether the plane was ready to go or not. The officials had earlier tentatively approved the plane but expressed the feeling that its fuel supply was marginal. They suggested that the crew add additional tankage if they wished to remain in the race. Tannus had answered that the qualification test had been conducted against a headwind using low-octane fuel. He felt the headwind cut their speed by five miles per hour, and the low-octane fuel cost them another seven miles per hour. But the race committee was not persuaded.

Late in the day the Gideon Society gave each pilot a Bible. Augy Pedlar denied reports that Mildred Doran was considering dropping out as a passenger. He told reporters that carrying her as a passenger was in his contract with Bill Malloska, and he intended to stick to it.

All nine planes were rolled out to their proper positions on the field, with the *Oklahoma* at the starting line and the others forming a semicircle approximately 200 feet behind it. Guards were placed around the airplanes to be sure that no damage occurred and that no curiosity-seekers would try to obtain last minute souvenirs. It was also not beyond belief that some one of the contestants might try to better his own chances at the expense of one of his fellows. Competition was increasing and tension was rising.

"As the sun sank slowly in the west" on Monday evening each pilot and navigator was filled with his own private thoughts. Each wondered if he would see his next sunset far out over the Pacific. After many hectic weeks, a calm settled over the Oakland airport. Most of the crews had a quiet dinner and retired to their hotel rooms in San Francisco.

The stage was set for the day of days, Tuesday, 16 August 1927.

7

HAWAII PREPARES

As the starting date of the Pacific Air Race approached, the people of San Francisco and Oakland were not the only ones caught up in the enthusiasm. Plans were being made in Honolulu for a lavish reception for the race pilots and navigators upon their arrival at Wheeler Field. The race was shaping up as the biggest event in recent history for the Hawaiian Islands, and the local businessmen, politicians, and military leaders were all determined to make the most of it. Many of them agreed with the thoughts, previously expressed by James Dole, that Hawaii's future would be based on air travel and that they should all do what they could to promote the race and Hawaii's part in it.

After Commander Rodgers's flight in 1925 there had been a brief flurry of aviation activity in the islands. Some enthusiasts immediately started to talk of the coming days when aerial service would be established between the mainland and the islands, and mail and passengers would be routinely whisked across the Pacific between dawn and dusk. Others, more practical, realized that the establishment of interisland aerial service should come first and started to work toward that end. They reasoned that island residents would have to be exposed to aerial travel to stimulate public acceptance, which in turn would attract the necessary capital investment. Airports were started in Honolulu, Hilo, and Maui. Army Air Service squadrons were based in Hawaii and numerous interisland flights were made.

On 30 January 1927 Edwin H. Lewis established a flying service devoted principally to passenger-hopping on Sunday afternoons with an occasional round-the-islands or interisland flight whenever a paying passenger wanted to go. Lewis purchased a three-place, open-cockpit, Ryan monoplane and had it converted to a five-place, closed-cabin monoplane. Marty Jensen had agreed to come to Hawaii with the plane. Already he was toying with the idea of flying from the mainland to the islands.

But the spark of enthusiasm for aerial travel in Hawaii seemed destined to die before it was even given a chance to grow, for by April 1927, the Lewis Aerial Tours Company was almost broke. Then Lindbergh made his famous flight. That flight and the immediate follow-up offer by Dole reawakened Hawaiians to the possibility of air travel and resulted in a new lease on life for Lewis Aerial Tours.

The people of Hawaii were determined to keep up their reputation for friendliness by showing the world how visiting fliers should be welcomed. The Aloha Committee of the Honolulu Chamber of Commerce was in charge of all arrangements for receptions and entertainment for the participants. On Monday, 8 August, a meeting was held to finalize arrangements for all of the activities being planned. Transportation for the arriving fliers and welcoming dignitaries from Wheeler Field to the Waikiki Beach area would be provided. The Royal Hawaiian Hotel, less than a year old but already famous as one of the most elegant and beautiful hotels in the world, was selected as official headquarters. Dole agreed to act as host and offered to pay all the fliers' expenses, including hotel accomodations, for four or five days after their arrival.

Optimism was the order of the day. Apparently few people realized the dangers associated with the flight, or if they did, they were not talking about them. The Aloha Committee estimated that ten airplanes would be arriving at various times of the day starting as early as 3:00 A.M. Saturday, 13 August, and probably ending about 11:00 A.M. These estimates, apparently based on average flying speeds of 100 to 130 miles per hour for a total of 18 to 24 hours, were extremely optimistic. No one took into account that, even under favorable conditions, very few of the heavily loaded aircraft were capable of maintaining cruising speeds of 100 or more miles per hour. Most of the planes, such as the Breese models flown by Jensen and Irving and the Travel Airs flown by Griffin and Goebel, would cruise somewhat below 80 miles per hour initially, slowly accelerating to about 90 or 95 miles per hour as the fuel is used up and they become lighter. Thus they could not be expected to arrive before early afternoon. Also the time that could be lost due to adverse winds, even if they averaged only 10 miles per hour, could add an additional two or three hours to the flight time. The prevailing winds over the Pacific were usually from the west to east, and 10 miles per hour would certainly not be a high estimate. In spite of these facts a luncheon was scheduled for Saturday, 13 August, in hopes the fliers would arrive by that time.

Twelve automobiles, each holding four or more passengers, were to be held in readiness at Wheeler Field to provide transportation for the fliers as they arrived. Special reviewing stands for the more prominent visitors were under construction and the Army personnel from Schofield Barracks were busily engaged in preparing parking areas for a total of 8,000 cars. Refreshment stands were being built as it was anticipated that the crowds of well-wishers would arrive early and stay late, starting during the evening of 12 August and continuing through the morning and afternoon of 13 August. Bleacher seats for 1,600 people were planned with an admittance charge to the area of 10 cents per person. All receipts would be donated to the Army Recreational Fund.

As the local newspapers increased their publicity and interest began to build up it was decided that seats for more than 1,600 people would be needed. Bleacher-seat capacity was increased to 3,000, and the fee was raised to 25 cents per person. In addition, special facilities were being prepared for the soldiers and their families that normally lived at Schofield Barracks. Many festivities were planned for the days following the fliers' arrival. It was realized that after the initial flurry of excitement, speeches, congratulations, and picture-taking sessions on Saturday, 13 August, the fliers would need and appreciate a good rest. No formal festivities were planned for Saturday or Sunday, but a gigantic reception consisting of a dinner and dance would be held on Monday evening, 15 August. This was to be held at the Royal Hawaiian Hotel with dinner scheduled at 7:00 P.M., a reception at 8:15 P.M., followed by the dance at 9:30 P.M. Admission was $2.50, and the event was open to the public. Those who could not attend the dinner were invited to the reception, which was complimentary. However, for visitors who did not attend the dinner but wished to attend the dance a cover charge of $1.00 would be collected. Initial interest was such that a sell-out crowd was expected, assuring the fliers a royal welcome.

Invitations were issued to many dignitaries and reserved seating was provided in the stands at Wheeler Field. Among those expected to attend were Governor Wallace Farrington and his party, James D. Dole's party, members of the flight committee, and local Air Service, Army, and Navy officers.

A few of the backers and close friends of the fliers were already waiting at Honolulu to greet the entrants. Marty Jensen's wife was still in Hawaii, where she continued to raise funds to back her husband's attempt. Bill Malloska, owner and sponsor of the *Miss Doran*, arrived on 9 August on the S. S. *Matsonia* and announced he had invested 30,000 dollars in the venture. He voiced the opinion that not more than half of the entrants would actually start the race. Events were to prove him right: only eight of the original fifteen reached the starting line. He stressed that his entrant was well prepared and not a last-minute decision as were many of the others. He had placed the down payment on the Buhl airplane the day before Lindbergh took off for Paris.

The local newspapers and some of those on the mainland were preparing to set up all-night vigils to keep the public informed of the fliers' progress. Many of the contestants were planning on using both sending and receiving radio sets. Between reports expected at frequent intervals direct from the fliers and reports of sightings along the route by the numerous Navy and commercial ships, the newsmen expected to be kept busy. The race was shaping up as one of the best-covered stories in recent times. Even before it started it was crowding many other major events off the front page.

Naturally Riley Allen and Joe Farrington, of the Honolulu *Star Bulletin*, were in the forefront of all the preparation. As the originators of the idea for the Pacific Air Race, they came in for their share of publicity, and they spearheaded their paper's efforts to publicize the fliers' arrival.

Late in the afternoon of Thursday, 11 August, word was received at Honolulu that the start of the race was to be postponed until noon, Pacific time, 16 August, to allow a larger number of pilots and planes to be qualified. This news meant the planes would be arriving on Wednesday, 17 August, and all the preparations for receptions and dinners were disrupted. After shuffling schedules, the same basic plans would be followed with the initial greetings on arrival Wednesday, a day of rest on Thursday, and a lavish reception, luau-style dinner, and dance on Friday, 19 August. This schedule would better fit the reception committee's plans, as they too were running late in their preparations. The reviewing stands could now be completed, the field prepared, and the festivities organized at a more leisurely pace.

Hawaii, already famed for its welcoming ceremonies, was preparing one of its greatest. As the day approached, 50,000 people made plans to greet the first mass flight to their shores. Every worker who could be spared would be given the day off. Most of the Army and Navy personnel were to be given leave, and all planned on spending the day at Wheeler Field. Six to eight thousand cars were expected to be parked at the field, which must have included almost every automobile on the island of Oahu. The Army Air Service planned to keep a number of planes in the air starting at dawn, to spot the arriving fliers and escort them to the field. With less than a week to go all Hawaii was almost ready.

Except Will Scott, a bakery manager for the Metropolitan Meat Market of Honolulu. Scott had one final detail to complete, and he was hard at work. He was baking, or building, a huge cake to commemorate the finish of the Dole race. It was to be 18 inches in diameter with twelve supporting pillars and a top layer consisting of mountains, a house, a waterfall, and a small model airplane. A tiny electric light simulated moonlight. On one side was a miniature grand piano with sheet music titled "Dole Plantation." The icing was gold adorned with white and yellow roses. When Scott finished his masterpiece he placed it on display in the meat market window.

Now Hawaii was ready.

8

GET SET

Tuesday, 16 August 1927 dawned the same as practically any other August day in Oakland, California. Weather reports were good with no major storms reported between Oakland and the Hawaiian Islands. However, in 1927 there were no satellites or sophisticated weather reporting stations covering the Pacific, so most forecasts for the area 100 miles past the shoreline were educated guesses based on sketchy reports from ships at sea. The forecast called for a light headwind for about 500 miles to longitude 130.° At about 140° northeast trade winds should be encountered at about 1,000 feet of altitude, which should provide a partial tailwind all the way to Hawaii. The ceiling at the airport was about 400 feet and the San Francisco Bay area and the Golden Gate were obscured by fog and haze, which was expected to clear by noon.

The Navy announced their biggest, best, and only aircraft carrier, U.S.S. *Langley,* and the aircraft tender, U.S.S. *Aroostook,* were in readiness at San Francisco, if needed. At that time, these two vessels represented almost the entire Naval Air Arm. Three destroyers, *Hazelwood, Meyer,* and *Sumner,* were on station at 100, 200, and 400 miles respectively from San Francisco. Four others, including *McDonough,* were cruising approximately midway between San Francisco and Hawaii. The Navy was being most cooperative in unofficial support of the Pacific Air Race, welcoming the opportunity to obtain favorable publicity to offset that recently received by the Army Air Service for Lieutenants Maitland and Hegenberger and their flight across the Pacific a few months earlier.

The Matson Steamship Company issued instructions to the captains of two of their liners, the S. S. *Manukai* and S. S. *Manulani,* to flash their searchlights three times every ten minutes throughout the night to serve as beacons for the fliers. The beams were to be aimed at an elevation from five to ten degrees above the eastern horizon. The S. S. *Manulani* was approximately 1,000 miles and the S. S. *Manukai* 1,280 miles west of San Francisco.

Early in the morning the crowds began to arrive at the Oakland Airport. By 9:00 A.M. long lines of cars extended from downtown Oakland to the airport parking lots. A festive air was evident with refreshment stands and souvenir salesmen doing a brisk business. During the early hours, before the crowds became too large, the people were allowed to wander around the field inspecting their favorite airplanes, watching the preparations, talking to the crews, and asking the standard questions over and over. How fast do you fly? How high do you fly? Why do you fly? When will you get to Hawaii?

The various race officials, local dignitaries, politicians needing publicity, and just plain people stood beside the airplanes while someone snapped their picture with the popular Kodak or Graphic camera. Members of the press went from one plane to another hoping to get some last-minute quote for the next deadline. All the papers in the area were prepared to release a special edition as soon as the race started.

Nine airplanes in various stages of readiness were arranged in a semicircle at the edge of the field. Each one had its own group of crew members and interested bystanders helping or hindering in the preparations. Engines were repeatedly started and stopped, adjusted and restarted. The planes had previously been moved to the starting area, which was marked off with liberal amounts of chalk. The actual starting line was flanked by lines indicating where the newsmen and photographers were allowed to stand. Behind these lines were fences that separated the public from the starting area. The fences extended the length of the runway to insure that a cleared area would be available for takeoff.

Clarence W. Young, who on 1 July had been appointed chief of the newly formed Civil Aeronautics Division of the Department of Commerce, was on hand to supervise the proceedings. Walter Beech had been in the area for the past few days to keep an eye on his company's two Travel Airs, *Oklahoma* and *Woolaroc*. Ken Boedecker of the Wright Aeronautical Company was nervously rushing from plane to plane with last minute hints and a helping hand. Now that the field was down to nine entrants the Wright J–5 engine was being used in all the aircraft. This was quite a feather in the cap of Wright Aeronautical as it certainly indicated strong faith in the engine. Bryce Goldsborough of the Pioneer Instrument Company was unable to keep up with the many requests for his help. All of the entrants were using at least a few of the long line of Pioneer instruments, principally the newly developed earth inductor compass, and each one wanted some last minute advice or help. Billy Parker was trying to help Art Goebel with his last-minute preparations. Goebel seemed to become more nervous with each passing minute, and Parker spent most of his time trying to reassure him and calm him down.

About two hours before the race was scheduled to begin, Parker flew out past the Golden Gate in his Travel Air biplane to check the fog bank that was still hanging over the area. He climbed up through it and found clear skies at about 2,000 feet. Returning, he advised Goebel to circle San Francisco while climbing above the fog. Parker rightly guessed that most of the pilots with their heavily loaded planes would try to stay below the fog hoping to leave it behind by nightfall. Getting above it right at the start could be an advantage in the long run, especially if the fog bank did not disappear before dark. Bill Erwin reportedly took his *Dallas Spirit* up for two short flights before the race for last-minute checks.

Jack Frost walked around the starting line in his bow tie and white checkered plus fours, the picture of a sportsman pilot. Gordon Scott, navigator for Frost, was also a snappy dresser and with his curly hair and youthful grin appeared to be headed for an afternoon of golf rather than a grueling flight to Hawaii. Scott, however, was trying hard not to show his concern. His brother, Denham, had spent the night sitting in the cockpit of the *Golden Eagle* to guard it from intruders. Police had been stationed throughout the area where the competing aircraft were parked, but most of the contestants added their own guards in and around their planes. During the night one of the policemen told Denham Scott that three men from the Pioneer Instrument Company were ready to check the instruments. As Ken Jay and Jack Frost had told Denham that absolutely no one was to be allowed on board the *Golden Eagle*, Denham refused to allow the men inside. The police told the visitors to leave, and nothing more was heard from them. The next morning, when Denham told his brother of the incident, Scott and Jay checked with Bryce Goldsborough of Pioneer Instrument Company, who denied having sent anyone to their plane during the night. Frost and Scott both tried to dismiss the incident from their minds, but still they couldn't help but wonder if someone was trying to sabotage the *Golden Eagle*. Scott was also toying with the idea of eliminating the radio to save weight. He checked with Jack Northrop, who pulled out his ever-present slide rule and quickly computed the real savings would be in the elimination of drag produced by the long aerial needed for the sending set. It came out to an increase of three miles per hour. Scott stated "We're in a race" and decided to eliminate the heavy transmitter and aerial. He substituted a lightweight receiver, which did not require the long aerial but which would still allow them to receive signals as they approached Hawaii. Both Scott and Frost, though they had an excellent plane, knew the penalty of each extra pound of weight and ounce of drag and were trying to eliminate as much of each as possible.

Throughout the entire morning a huge road grader had been slowly wending its way from one end of the 7,000-foot runway to the other. No planes had been allowed to use the main runway since the preceding evening to be sure that no imperfections in the surface would mar a contestant's takeoff. With the fuel and equipment loads carried by each plane they could not afford the usual bumps of a typical 1927 airport.

Arguments continued between the race officials and the *City of Peoria* crew and backers. Apparently it still was not decided whether the *City of Peoria* would be finally approved, nor could anyone determine if Parkhurst and Lowes were really going to fly it. S. F. Tannus was still threatening to turn the plane over to a new crew, but the race committee issued a statement that they would not allow any further pilot or navigator substitutions.

Most of the crowd's interest centered on the *Miss Doran*. The plane with its brillant red, white, and blue color scheme stood out among the entrants. Then too, this was the only entrant that would carry a passenger, the young schoolteacher, Mildred Doran. She had been basking in the attention of the press and her new-found friends of the past few weeks. When she arrived at the field about 9:30 A.M. she was dressed in an olive drab flying costume with golf stockings and a leather helmet. When asked if she wasn't afraid of the coming flight she said, "I'm not a bit worried about the flight although I suppose I should be." The pilot, Augy Pedlar, was dressed in a sport shirt and his usual straw hat. He too seemed to be enjoying the adulation of the crowd, signing autographs and thanking people for their well wishes.

At about 10:00 A.M. it appeared that nine planes, seventeen men, and one girl were more or less ready to depart. Except one plane, the *City of Peoria*, was still the center of controversy. Between 10:00 and 11:00 the race officials finally reached a decision and at 11:15 issued an announcement that, though shocking, was not really unexpected. Rumors had been flying since Monday and the crew had been previously warned that if they did not increase their gasoline capacity they could be disqualified. Now a formal notice was handed to Charlie Parkhurst that stated "We consider this plane has insufficient gasoline capacity for the required mileage." Tannus was most outspoken in his objections and let everyone within earshot hear his opinion of the race committee, the Civil Aeronautics Division of the Department of Commerce, and even a few of the other contestants. But the committee had many things to do, time was running out, and the decision was final.

Surprisingly Parkhurst and Lowes offered only mild objections. Underneath it all they appeared to be relieved that the decision was made and they no longer could be held responsible.

With less than an hour to go before the starting gun, the pace of the preparations started to increase. A group of thirty men, under the command of Capt. Burdette A. Palmer of the Air Corps Reserve, was designated as a "Crash Detail" and took their places along the 7,000-foot runway. The area adjacent to the runway was cleared of spectators, and everyone was repeatedly warned to remain behind the fences. Some of the members of the "Crash Detail" were equipped with cars, and a number of ambulances were strategically placed near the far end of the runway to be available at or near the point of takeoff. Most of the pilots, by this time, were in their cockpits checking, for at least the tenth time, their emergency equipment, food supplies, and in most cases their personal rabbit's foot or similar talisman.

The committee realized they couldn't stop Oakland and San Francisco pilots from following the racers out over the city, but they did announce that all airplanes in the air at the start of the race must maintain at least 300 feet of clearance from the racers. Many of the local pilots were already in the air planning to escort their favorite entry out at least a few miles over the Pacific. One last check was made of the crowd and the last stragglers were herded back behind the fences, approximately 500 feet from the starting line. The planes were grouped in a semicircle, except for the *Oklahoma*, which had already been taxied up to the line. Now with only a few minutes to go each pilot and navigator had his own private thoughts. Most of them gave little evidence of their true feelings or the excitement that was building up within them. Mildred Doran seemed to be losing some of her girlish enthusiasm, but she climbed aboard the *Miss Doran* and settled down for a long ride.

Benny Griffin appeared to be somewhat disturbed as he and navigator Al Henley checked over their plane. To the knowledgeable bystander this was a bad omen; Benny had always been a steady, unruffled, confident pilot, completely sure of himself and his ability. Few people knew about Ken Boedecker's warning that the Phillips fuel might produce too high a cylinder-head temperature in the Wright J–5. Boedecker did not say the Phillips fuel should not be used, but he did urge Griffin to be extremely careful of operating his engine at full throttle especially on the ground, and to keep his eyes open for any sign of overheating. Griffin was worrying that Boedecker was right and that the ground testing and run-up might have already had an adverse effect on his engine.

When Boedecker again came over to see how Griffin was progressing, the pilot asked him if he would care to ride along to Hawaii. Griffin felt that having the best engine service man in the business with him might help. But Boedecker was not interested in the role of passenger. His entire effort was directed toward getting all nine aircraft safely off the ground, each with a smooth-running Wright J–5 engine.

Livingston Irving was beginning to appreciate the immensity of the job ahead of him, acting as both pilot and navigator on the flight. His wife

Cmdr. Rodgers in the PN-9 flying boat leaving San Francisco Bay for Honolulu, 31 Aug. 1925 *(Smithsonian Institution)*

Travel MA being modified for use by Smith and Carter for their Pacific flight. Wording on coveralls of the mechanics reads "Trans Pacific Flight Honolulu" *(Eddie Cooper)*

The James D. Dole $35,000 Prizes

North America---Honolulu, Hawaii
Trans-Pacific Flight

National Aeronautic Association, Honolulu Chapter, Honolulu, Hawaii

(Under the competition rules of the National Aeronautic Association of the United States of America, the Fédération Aéronautique Internationale of Paris, France, and the special regulations of the Contest Committee of the Honolulu Chapter, National Aeronautic Association.)

Prizes of $25,000 and $10,000 have been offered by Mr. James D. Dole of Honolulu, to be awarded to the first and second aviators respectively who shall cross the Pacific in a land or water aircraft (heavier than air) from the North American continent to Honolulu, Hawaii, without stop, within one year from August 12, 1927.

QUALIFICATIONS OF COMPETITORS—The competition is open to aviators of allied nationality holding an F. A. I. certificate (land plane or seaplane) and annual sporting license issued by a National Federation affiliated with the Fédération Aéronautique Internationale and duly entered in the competitors' register of the National Aeronautic Association.

ENTRIES—The Entry Form for the flight, which must be accompanied by the Entrance Fee of $100, must be sent to the Starting Committee at the San Francisco Chapter, National Aeronautic Association, San Francisco, at least ten days prior to intended date of take-off, and a copy thereof sent to the Contest Committee, National Aeronautic Association, Honolulu Chapter, Honolulu, Hawaii, at the same time.

No part of the entrance fee is to be received by Mr. James D. Dole, the donor. All amounts received will be applied toward payment of the expenses of conducting the competition.

STARTING TIME—The start may be made at any time after noon, Pacific time, Friday, August 12, 1927, for a period of one year thereafter.

STARTING PLACE—Point of departure to be any point on the North American Continent. Competitors should indicate definitely to the starting committee their point of take-off.

FINISH—Finish for land planes to be at the John Rodgers Airport, located four miles west of Honolulu, and for seaplanes at Pearl Harbor, located eight miles west of Honolulu, although a landing at any place on the island of Oahu will be considered as a finish.

A map showing the location of the finish and all landing fields in the Hawaiian Islands will be furnished each competitor.

The start or landing may be made from land or water. All starts must be made under the supervision of the Starting Committee or an Official or Officials appointed by that Committee. The time will be taken from the moment of leaving the selected starting place, in case of land planes. For starts made from the water, the time of start and finish will be taken from the moment of leaving and reaching land or crossing the finish line. In each case the pilot must report in person to the Starting Committee or its representatives at the start, and to the Contest Committee at the finish.

ROUTE—The route shall be via the established steamer lanes, great circle courses, from the Continent to Honolulu.

TYPE OF MACHINES ELIGIBLE—Any type of land plane or seaplane suitably constructed and equipped, is eligible. Only the aircraft registered, or one of identical type and construction, may be used under each entry blank filed.

All planes shall be so marked before starting that they may be readily identified en route and on reaching Honolulu.

The Starting Committee or its representatives will require demonstrations of air-worthiness, navigability and equipment of all entries.

FUEL—The aircraft shall be provided with the necessary tank capacity and shall carry at the start, fuel and oil, fifteen (15) per cent in excess of that actually required for the flight.
The gasoline tanks must be sealed with the seal of the officials in control at the starting point, and the seals shall remain intact when reaching Honolulu, and subject to the inspection of Officials in control.

All planes shall carry a barograph which must be sealed with the seal of the Officials in control at the starting point and this seal must be intact when it reaches Honolulu.

SAFETY REQUIREMENTS:

Flotation—Suitable life-float or floats shall be carried capable of sustaining the crew of the plane.

Sustenance—Sufficient food and water shall be carried for three days.

Visual Signals—Ten (10) smoke flares or candles shall be carried.

Radio—A small semi-automatic code signaling set. This item is recommended but is not mandatory.

GENERAL

1. A competitor, by entering, thereby agrees that he is bound by the Regulations herein contained, or to be hereafter issued in connection with this competition.

2. The interpretation of these Regulations, or any to be hereafter issued, shall rest entirely with the Contest and Starting Committees and delegated Officials.

3. The competitor shall be solely responsible to the Officials for the due observance of these Regulations, and shall be the person with whom the Officials will deal in respect thereof, or of any other question arising out of this competition.

4. A competitor, by entering, waives, any right of action against the National Aeronautic Association for any damages sustained by him in consequence of any act or omission on the part of the Officials of the National Aeronautic Association of the United States of America, the Contest and Starting Committee Officials of the James D. Dole $35,000 Prizes and/or Mr. James D. Dole, the donor, or their representatives or servants, or any fellow competitor.

...time... ...risk in all respects of... ...who sh... ...waive all cla... ...ury either to himself or his pass... ...or his ...orkmen, and to assume all liability for damage... ...ties... and to indemnify the National Aeronautic Association, the Contest and... James D. Dole, the donor, in respect thereof.

6. The Contest Committee of the Honolulu Chapter, National Aeronautic Association for the James D. Dole Prize Flight reserve to themselves the right, with the consent of Mr. James D. Dole, to add to, amend or omit any of these rules should they deem it advisable.

7. The entry for each attempt with certified check for $100, payable to the Treasurer, Honolulu Chapter, N. A. A., must be received by the Starting Committee at the San Francisco Chapter, N. A. A., at San Francisco, not later than ten days before the intended date of take-off for the flight.

JAMES D. DOLE $35,000 PRIZES

CONTEST COMMITTEE

CHAIRMAN

CLARENCE H. COOKE,
President, Honolulu Chapter, National Aeronautic Association; President, Bank of Hawaii, Honolulu.

MEMBERS

FRANK O. BOYER,
Director, Honolulu Chapter, National Aeronautic Association.

Lieut.-Comdr. M. B. McCOMB, U.S.N.,
Commanding Officer, Naval Air Station, Pearl Harbor, Hawaii.

Capt. LOWELL H. SMITH, U.S.A.
Commander 19th Pursuit Squadron, Wheeler Field, Hawaii.

TREASURER

THEODORE A. COOKE,
Treasurer, Honolulu Chapter, National Aeronautic Association.

SECRETARY

JOHN H. KANGETER,
Secretary, Honolulu Chapter, National Aeronautic Association.

ADVISORY MEMBERS

A. W. VAN VALKENBURG,
Chairman, Airways and Landing Field Committee, Honolulu Chapter, National Aeronautic Association. Secretary Oahu Railway and Land Company, Honolulu.

KENNETH B. BARNES,
Director, Honolulu Chapter, National Aeronautic Association; Secretary and Director of Hawaiian Pineapple Company, Honolulu, Hawaii.

STARTING COMMITTEE

CHAIRMAN

Capt. C. W. SAUNDERS,
National Aeronautic Association Governor for California; Operating Manager, Matson Navigation Company, San Francisco.

HARRY E. MacCONAUGHEY,
Vice-President and San Francisco Manager, Hawaiian Pineapple Company, San Francisco.

VALENTINE GEPHART,
Secretary, National Aeronautic Association of the United States, Seattle, Washington.

HARRY CHANDLER,
President and General Manager,
The Los Angeles Times, Los Angeles.

COUNSEL
PROSSER, ANDERSON & MARX,
Honolulu, Hawaii.

CUSTODIAN AND DEPOSITARY
BANK OF HAWAII,
Honolulu, Hawaii.

The James D. Dole $35,000 Prizes
NORTH AMERICA—HONOLULU, HAWAII
Trans-Pacific Flight

(Under the rules of the Fédération Aéronautic Internationale, Paris, France, National Aeronautic Association of the United States of America, and the special Regulations of the Contest Committee of the Honolulu Chapter, National Aeronautic Association, Honolulu, Hawaii).

ENTRY FORM

Name of Aviator Entrant (in full) ....

Address ....

Aviator's F. A. I. Certificate No. .... Issued by ....

Aviator's Annual License No. .... Issued by ....

PARTICULARS RELATING TO THE AIRCRAFT INTENDED TO BE USED:

....

....

Type (Monoplane, Biplane, Hydroaeroplane, Flying Boat, etc.) ....

....

Wing area in sq. feet .... Load per sq. feet ....

Make and type of engine .... Cu. in. Disp. ....

Approximate capacity of Fuel Tanks ....

    I, the undersigned .... of .... hereby enter for the James D. Dole North America-Honolulu $35,000 prizes, upon the following conditions:

    1. I agree to observe and abide by the Rules and Regulations for the time being in force and governing the contest, and to comply in all respects and at all times with the requests or instructions regarding the contest, which may be given to me by any of the Officials of the Starting Committee of the James D. Dole Flight.

    2. In addition to, and not by way of, limitation of the liabilities assumed by me by this entry under the said Rules and Regulations, I agree also to indemnify the National Aeronautic Association of the United States of America and the Contest and Starting Committees of the James D. Dole $35,000 Prizes, and Mr. James D. Dole, the donor of the North America-Honolulu, Hawaii, trans-Pacific flight, or their representatives or servants, or any fellow competitor, against all claims and damages arising out of, or caused by, any ascent, flight or descent made by me, whether or not such claims and demands shall arise directly out of my own actions or out of the acts, actions, or proceedings of any persons assembling to witness or be present at such ascent or descent.

    3. I enclose my certified check for $100 to the order of the Treasurer of the Honolulu Chapter, National Aeronautic Association, being entrance fee for the James D. Dole $35,000 Prizes, and request to be entered on the Competitors' Register of the National Aeronautic Association of the United States of America.

                                            Signature ....

                                            Address ....

(Notary Seal.)

Date ....

    This blank is to be executed in duplicate and forwarded with certified check and original to the Starting Committee at the San Francisco Chapter, National Aeronautic Association, San Francisco; and the duplicate copy forwarded immediately to the Contest Committee of the Honolulu Chapter, National Aeronautic Association, Honolulu, Hawaii.

Drawing for starting times for the Dole race. Names were drawn from a waste basket *(Marty Jensen)*

Al Henley, left, Benny Griffin, center, and unidentified friend in front of *Oklahoma (Ralph Brown through Pete Westburg)*

Right front view of *Oklahoma* at Oakland Airport shortly before start of the race. Note small square panel on fuselage that reads "Phillips Nu-Aviation Gasoline" *(Dole Co.)*

Installing belly tank during rebuilding of *El Encanto (San Diego Museum)*

Ken Hawkins, left, and Norm Goddard, right, in front of *El Encanto* at Oakland. Final alterations not complete as belly tank not yet sealed and airspeed Pitot tube not yet installed on right lift strut *(San Diego Museum)*

Left front view of *City of Peoria* warming up *(Ralph Brown through Pete Westburg)*

Right front view of *City of Peoria*. Second from left with helmet is Charlie Parkhurst, third from left, Ralph Lowes. Other two men unidentified but believed to be Standard Red Crown representatives *(Ralph Brown through Pete Westburg)*

Miss Doran having compass "swung" at Oakland prior to race *(Dole Co.)*

Mildred Doran, passenger, and Vilas Knope, navigator, shortly before start of race. *Golden Eagle* is in the background *(Denham Scott)*

Pilot Augy Pedlar, left, and Vilas Knope, right, in front of *Miss Doran* *(Ralph Brown through Pete Westburg)*

Bill Erwin, pilot of the *Dallas Spirit* *(Aerograph Co.)*

Dallas Spirit being run up a few days before the race *(Ralph Brown through Pete Westburg)*

Pabco Pacific Flyer on the line awaiting start of the race *(Dole Co.)*

Pride of Los Angeles after conversion to Wright J–5 engines *(Aerograph Co.)*

Art Goebel at nose of *Woolaroc* before leaving the Travel Air factory *(Ralph Brown through Pete Westburg)*

Walter Beech, left, and Art Goebel, right, in front of the *Woolaroc* at the Travel Air factory *(Beech Aircraft)*

Frank Phillips, left, and Art Goebel, right, in front of *Woolaroc* after it was rebuilt and returned to Oklahoma *(T. Wadlow)*

Woolaroc and the Travel Air group that helped build it. Left to right: Walter Burnham, Herb Rawdon, William "Frenchy" Hauselman, Pinky Grimes, Ted Cochran, Art Goebel, Ralph Morton, Harold Brooks, H. E. Weimiller, Clarence Clark *(Beech Aircraft)*

Woolaroc at Travel Air factory *(Beech Aircraft through Russ Plehinger)*

Aloha at Oakland prior to the race *(Russ Plehinger)*

Left 1/4 view of *Hummingbird*. Note lack of forward vision and lack of dihedral in wings *(San Diego Museum)*

Left 3/4 view of *Hummingbird* with George Covell, Richard Waggener, and an unidentified mechanic at San Diego. Note lack of forward vision from cockpit *(San Diego Museum)*

Golden Eagle ready to take off on its first test flight *(Smithsonian Institution)*

Gordon Scott, left, and Jack Frost, right, under wing of *Golden Eagle* a few days before the race. Note navigator window in wing and no evidence of fuselage damage *(Denham Scott)*

Jack Frost in cockpit of *Golden Eagle* shortly before the race. Crack in fuselage ahead of landing gear can be seen in this view *(Ralph Brown through Pete Westburg)*

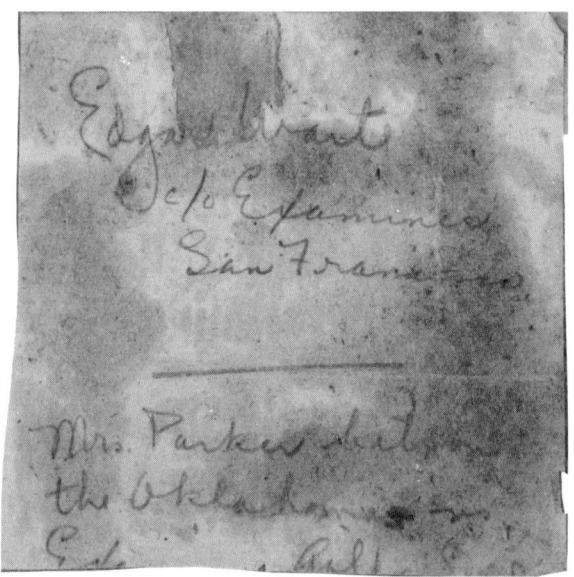

Note reading "Edgar Wait c/o Examiner San Francisco. Mrs. Parker bets on the Oklahoma in Examiner pool" *(Billy Parker)*

Close up, right side of *City of Peoria*. Note extremely short fuselage and large vertical stabilizer *(Ralph Brown through Pete Westburg)*

Pride of Los Angeles after crash at Oakland. All occupants escaped with little injury, but the plane was a total loss. Water appears about 2 to 3 feet deep *(Aerograph Co.)*

Right front view of *City of Peoria* being fueled *(Ralph Brown through Pete Westburg)*

Miss Doran being topped off with fuel just before start of race. Note gasoline is being filtered as it is pumped into the fuselage tank. Also an opening has been cut in the cabin roof for the navigator, and drift lines are evident on the horizontal stabilizer *(Dole Co.)*

Left front view of *Miss Doran*. Plane appears ready to take off as well-wishers say their final good-byes *(San Diego Museum)*

Shelia Scott kissing her brother Gordon good-bye before start of race. Their brother Denham watches. All three are at the tail of the *Golden Eagle* *(Denham Scott)*

Composite photo of the actual start of the race with the flag dropping and the ground crew helping the *Oklahoma* to roll *(Benny Griffin)*

Takeoff of *Oklahoma*. Note ambulances located along runway *(Dole Co.)*

El Encanto at Oakland shortly before race. Compass is being "swung" and plane is completely modified *(Dole Co.)*

Aerial view of damaged *El Encanto* after crowds had left. Guards are stationed around the plane *(Aerograph Co.)*

Golden Eagle on takeoff already 60 feet in the air at the point where most others had not yet left the ground. The crashed *El Encanto* lies on its side in the background *(Dole Co.)*

Actual takeoff of *Miss Doran (Dole Co.)*

Aloha at starting line ready to go *(Dole Co.)*

Woolaroc, actual start of the race *(Dole Co.)*

Actual takeoff of *Woolaroc* at start of race *(Dole Co. through Russ Plehinger)*

Dallas Spirit shortly before takeoff in the race *(Dole Co.)*

Right rear view of fuselage of *Dallas Spirit* after return to Oakland. Fabric on side has been cut away. Note both side and bottom are damaged *(Aerograph Co.)*

Pabco Pacific Flyer shortly after crash on takeoff. Mechanics' coveralls are marked "Breese Aircraft" *Ralph Brown through Pete Westburg)*

Telegram received by Billy Parker at end of race. It reads "3:05 P.M. Aug 17 19 Mr. Parker Room 5039 Your flying Wolrac arrived at Wheeler Field Pac Standard time 2:45 Aloha 2'nd in sight about 2 miles out. Opr. 11" *(Billy Parker)*

Bill Davis, left, and Art Goebel, right, in front of the *Woolaroc* at Oakland *(Ralph Brown through Pete Westburg)*

Copy of telegram sent to Billy Parker by Art Goebel after the race. It reads "Billy Parker, Palace Hotel, San Francisco. Philips new aviation gasoline certainly proved itself in the San Francisco Honolulu Air Race. I highly recommend it for Wright Engine flying time twenty six hours gas consumption 317 gallons. Art Goebel" *(Billy Parker)*

Aloha immediately after landing at Honolulu *(Smithsonian Institution)*

Mrs. Marty Jensen and James Dole at award presentation ceremonies. Note black armbands due to missing fliers *(Dole Co.)*

Bill Erwin on left beside the *Dallas Spirit (Ralph Brown through Pete Westburg)*

Aloha as rebuilt in Hawaii after the race *(Smithsonian Institution)*

Gordon Scott, left, and Jack Frost, right, in front of the *Golden Eagle* *(Eddie Cooper)*

Art Goebel in front of the *Woolaroc* after the plane had been refinished and the cockpit area rebuilt *(T. Wadlow)*

and daughter were most concerned, but Mrs. Irving tried her best not to show it.

The crew around the *Golden Eagle* appeared most relaxed. Eddie Cooper had completed his check list, every item had been crossed off. Shelia Scott posed for a picture kissing her brother good-bye, and Frost and Scott climbed aboard.

Most of the other pilots and navigators, though visibly nervous and anxious to get started, didn't appear to be particularly worried. Marty Jensen seemed especially relaxed even though he had spent a very hectic week preparing his plane. Though many of the various crew members had spent a sleepless night flying the race in advance, Jensen had slept well in his room at the Clift Hotel. He even surprised his navigator, Paul Schluter, who had shared the room with him and spent a fitful night anticipating his first long distance airplane ride. Both Jensen and Schluter expected to be quite hungry as they took a dozen sandwiches, a box of biscuits, six packs of chewing gum, and a dozen oranges. Thus fortified they both climbed into their respective cockpits and settled down in the *Aloha* to wait their turn to take off.

One entrant, Art Goebel, surprised the group around his plane. As the hours passed and the starting time of noon approached, he seemed to become more nervous and upset. As he made ready to climb into the cockpit, he hesitated and seemed almost on the verge of changing his mind. Billy Parker, who was the last person to talk to Goebel before he started his engine, said later that he noticed tears seemed to be forming in Goebel's eyes. In spite of Goebel's normal bravado and his years of stunt flying and barnstorming, when faced with the enormity of the Pacific, he appeared almost ready to give up. Parker, fearing the Phillips protegé would actually back out, spoke sharply to him and ridiculed him for his anxiety. Goebel apparently resigned himself to his fate and climbed into the cockpit. He was visibly shaken and still gave the appearance that for two cents he would give up the whole affair. Parker continued to pressure him, reminding him of his contract with Phillips and the fame and glory he could win. Once Goebel settled himself in the cockpit and started to check his supplies and equipment he seemed to get hold of himself and announced he was ready to go.

The minutes seemed to creep by for each contestant, but finally at 11:46 A.M. on a signal from E. Howard, official starter, Benny Griffin started the *Oklahoma*'s engine. As number one in the lineup the *Oklahoma* was already straddling the starting line. Griffin had earlier warmed up the engine so promptly at noon, as Howard waved the symbolic checkered flag, Griffin opened the throttle and the engine roared. The noise of the engine was almost drowned out by the combined roar of thousands of spectators.

The Pacific Air Race was on.

9

GO

It took almost a full minute to actually get the *Oklahoma* rolling due to its overloaded condition. With the help of some of the ground crew pushing hard on the wing struts, Benny Griffin's plane started to move slowly forward. As the plane started to roll the combined shouts of close to 75,000 people drowned out the roar of the engine. The first, the greatest, and what would prove to be the last transoceanic air race was underway. After a long but otherwise normal run, Griffin lifted the *Oklahoma* gently off the runway and started a long gentle climbing turn to the west toward downtown San Francisco and the Golden Gate.

The cheers from the crowds subsided, but as the next plane was pushed to the starting line the roar was repeated. At 12:02 P.M. the starting flag was again dipped and Norm Goddard in *El Encanto* started to roll. His plane, being somewhat lighter, got off to a faster start. About 2,600 to 3,000 feet down the runway Goddard tried to life the plane off, but *El Encanto* seemed to have a mind of its own, and it wasn't ready to fly. Goddard started to veer to the right, and the wheels started to dig into the soft earth of the runway border. The crowds, held back along the entire length of the runway by alert policemen, started to run away from the careening plane. The heavily loaded monoplane tipped toward the left as it left the runway causing the left wing to dig into the ground. A severe ground loop resulted. When the dust settled it could be seen the plane had made a half circle and had come to rest facing the starting line. Miraculously there was no sign of fire, though some of the fuel had spilled, and the police had to hold the crowd back from the damaged aircraft. One carelessly thrown cigarette could still cause a catastrophe. In a few seconds, even before the crowd could reach the plane, Goddard and Hawkins crawled out, unhurt, but the *El Encanto* was severely damaged. An argument immediately developed between Goddard and Hawkins with the pilot claiming the navigator had pushed the right rudder. Because the navigator's part of the cockpit allowed a better forward view than the pilot's Goddard had agreed to allow Hawkins to pilot the plane through the takeoff. Possibly this was a case of too many pilots spoiling the plane. Regardless of whose fault it was, most pilots in the audience were sure they knew what happened. Neither Goddard nor Hawkins had ever flown the *El Encanto* with its full fuel load. Not realizing how slow the fully loaded plane would pick up speed Goddard or Hawkins, or both, had tried to pull the plane off the ground prematurely, resulting in a partial stall. As one wing started to drop they tried to raise it using the aileron, and the increased drag of the lower aileron at slow speed caused the plane to roll, resulting in the ground loop. Fortunately the *El Encanto* was not blocking the runway so only a short delay ensued. Upon questioning, Hawkins stated, "I would rather have crashed in mid ocean than to have had this happen."

The next plane, the *Pabco Pacific Flyer*, had been pushed to the starting line, and the crew was nervously waiting for the runway to be cleared. Finally at 12:11 P.M. Livingston Irving started down the runway. After about 3,500 feet of roll the plane appeared to leave the ground but only for a few feet. It bounced back onto the runway rather hard. Irving apparently felt that he would not make it, cut his engine, and rolled to a stop. The tail skid was damaged slightly during one of the hard bounces, which made it difficult to move the heavy plane. It took 20 minutes to tow the plane clear of the runway. While it was being placed in a position where it would not be a hazard to the remaining contestants the next plane was pushed up to the starting line.

As soon as the *Golden Eagle* reached the starting line Jack Frost started the engine. But after about two minutes he realized there might be a long delay before the *Pabco Pacific Flyer* was moved so he shut off the engine and settled down to wait. He was confident. He knew his plane was the fastest in the field, so he could afford to lose a few minutes. At 12:28 P.M. the engine was restarted, and two minutes later the checkered flag fell again. Jack Frost and Gordon Scott roared down the runway and made what appeared to be the shortest and best takeoff of the entire group. At the 4,500-foot point on the runway they were already 60 feet in the air and climbing smoothly. By the time they cleared the end of the runway they had more than 200 feet of altitude. The *Golden Eagle* was living up to all of her maker's claims.

As Eddie Cooper watched the *Golden Eagle* rise effortlessly into the sky he couldn't contain himself. Rushing over to Jack Northrop and Ken Jay, with tears streaming down his cheeks, he shouted "I told you she'd make it! I told you my weight wouldn't make any difference! I told you!"

Years later in his home in California Eddie Cooper remembered how much he had wanted to be in the *Golden Eagle* on that takeoff, but he was thankful that Northrup and Jay saved his life when they refused to let him climb on board.

Next was the plane that most of the crowd had really come to see— the *Miss Doran*. The big red, white, and blue biplane had been waiting quite some time for its turn. At 12:33 P.M. the starter's flag dropped again and Augy Pedlar pushed forward on the throttle. Mildred Doran, having finally realized the die was cast, waved from her rear cabin section to the wildly cheering crowd. The big Buhl plane was not very streamlined and was slow getting started. It took practically all the runway but finally lumbered into the air and started a long slow climb to the west.

The starting committee, trying to regain some of the time that had been lost, had the next entry, *Aloha*, at the starting line even before the *Miss Doran* had left the ground. At 12:34 P.M. Marty Jensen and Paul Schluter roared down the runway and followed close behind the *Miss Doran* toward the Golden Gate. True to his plan Marty Jensen climbed just enough to clear the hills and buildings of San Francisco and started over the broad Pacific at about 50 or 60 feet above the water.

Keeping up the fast pace, the ground crew rapidly positioned the *Woolaroc* for takeoff. Two minutes later at 12:36 P.M. Art Goebel, having settled down from his prerace jitters, took off toward the Pacific without any trouble.

It only took one minute for Bill Erwin to taxi to the starting line and signal he was ready to go. He was given the checkered flag at 12:37 P.M. and started the *Dallas Spirit* straight down the runway. Almost effortlessly, the heavy plane, probably the heaviest in the race, lifted off and turned toward the Golden Gate.

As each contestant headed west they passed the heavily populated downtown San Francisco area. Every window of every house, store, and office building was filled with eager faces. Each balcony and roof, even some ledges, held groups of spectators. Most of the pilots climbed slowly and some were lower than the roofs of the downtown skyscrapers as they passed through the Golden Gate between the city and Sausalito across the bay.

It appeared that, after a few early mishaps, a race was underway. Of the nine entries that actually reached the starting circle eight started. The *El Encanto* had crashed without personnel injuries, the *Pabco Pacific Flyer* had aborted a takeoff and was even now being readied for another attempt, and six planes were on their way over the Pacific. Air traffic was rather heavy over the Golden Gate area as it seemed every private plane and many military planes were in the air, either circling over San Francisco Bay or following one of the contestants for a few miles over the ocean.

At 12:38 P.M. the race committee finally started to relax for the first time in months, and the crowd of 75,000 people started to get ready to go home. But just as a football game isn't over before the final gun, the Pacific Air Race wasn't over by a long shot. At 12:45 P.M., just eight minutes after the last plane had taken off, the *Oklahoma* reappeared over the airport. Smoke was trailing from the engine, and it was obvious that Benny Griffin was anxious to land. The ground crew and police had trouble clearing the runway but finally managed to open up an area large enough to use. Griffin quickly brought the plane in for a good landing even though it was still overloaded with more than 400 gallons of fuel. As the *Oklahoma* rolled to a stop, Al Henley could be seen standing in the navigator's cockpit with a fire extinguisher in his hand. The first reporters to reach the plane quoted him as saying, "The damned ship was burning up." Griffin and Henley jumped out quickly, and Griffin, in a highly excited state, started to give instructions to his ground crew. He hoped to have the *Oklahoma* repaired immediately and get back into the race. As soon as the mechanics were able to check the engine they determined that all nine cylinders were damaged to some extent. No valves had actually been swallowed, but many of the piston rings were sticking and probably the cylinder walls were scored or burned. After much arguing the normally calm and collected Griffin was forced to admit the *Oklahoma* was through for the day. There was no way an entire engine or engine cylinders could be changed and checked out in a short time even if the parts were available. Griffin talked to the press and gave a statement that he was withdrawing from the race, but he added that if none of the others made it to Hawaii he would try again in a few days. He then left the field, silent and dejected.

Reporters at the scene as well as later writers over the years built up the story that Benny Griffin was feuding with his navigator, Al Henley, because Henley had tested the engine excessively, causing the failure during the race. This story has no foundation in fact. As Benny Griffin recently remarked, "I wasn't the least bit mad at Al. If I had been, he sure wouldn't have been in the plane with me. All I can say is that Ken Boedecker was right."

While the crowd was still milling around the *Oklahoma*, another plane appeared overhead. The *Miss Doran* had returned, with the engine running rough, smoking and obviously in trouble. Unlike most of the entrants the *Miss Doran* was equipped with fuel dump valves, which allowed the pilot to dump overboard most of the fuel in case of an emergency. This not only lightened the load for landing but limited the amount of fuel that could spill in case of a crash-landing. Augy Pedlar had wisely flown out over the bay and dumped most of his fuel before attempting to land. He then made a good landing and taxied to the starting area. Immediately the ground crew started work on the engine. No major problems were found. A quick readjustment of the timing and a change of three spark plugs and the problem was solved.

Next the *Dallas Spirit* appeared over the field. It began to look like, one by one, all the entrants were returning. Long streamers of fabric were flapping around the tail assembly as Bill Erwin prepared to land. No one on the ground knew what the problem was, but it appeared serious. After a superb landing, Erwin discovered a large portion of the fuselage fabric had ripped loose leaving a gaping hole in the right rear and bottom of the fuselage. It was evident that the time required to repair the damage would put Erwin about three or four hours behind the leaders. He felt there would be little chance of making up that much lost time and therefore regretfully announced his withdrawal from the race.

Meanwhile the *Pabco Pacific Flyer* had been repaired, the engine run up, and all was declared in readiness. Buoyed up by the fact there were only three planes still in the race and none of them had more than a 45-minute lead, Livingston Irving decided to give it another try. He said good-bye to his wife and well-wishers for the second time, taxied up to the starting line, and signaled he was ready. At 1:20 P.M. they waved him off, and he started down the runway. After a reasonable run the *Flyer* left the ground and started to climb. Apparently not realizing how overloaded the plane was, Irving tried to pull it into a normal climb, but at about 50 feet of altitude it stalled and mushed back onto the runway with a resounding thud. The landing gear collapsed and the plane slid to a halt a short distance past the wrecked *El Encanto*. Again the familiar cloud of dust slowly settled while everyone held their breath. No fire. Irving's wife, Madeline, and his five-year-old daughter were among the first to reach the plane. They found Irving with a cut on his hand but otherwise uninjured, safe but disgusted that he had failed again. After thinking about it and talking to his wife he realized how fortunate he was to walk away from the crash. His wife and daughter were both overjoyed that the months of strain and tension were over. Madeline Irving summed it up when she said, "You've had quite a day. Let's go home".

By this time the ground crew of the *Miss Doran* had almost finished. Apparently, after seeing two crashes and a few near misses, Mildred Doran was beginning to realize the seriousness of flying the Pacific. In spite of the prerace hoopla, the adulation of the crowds and the wide publicity she had received in the press, when faced with the final go/no-go decision she burst into tears. What thoughts went through her mind will never be known, for Augy Pedlar was too busy getting ready for a second takeoff to pay much attention to a crying twenty-two-year-old girl. Mildred Doran was not in the mood to talk to reporters. Vilas Knope, who understood her fears, took her aside and earnestly tried to talk her into staying on the ground. By this time Mildred Doran really wanted to stay behind, but she feared humiliation more than the flight itself. Above all, she didn't want to disappoint Bill Malloska, who was even now waiting in Hawaii for word of the *Miss Doran*'s takeoff. After all, the flight had been her idea, and so many of her friends had invested so much time, effort, and money into it that she just couldn't let them down. Regardless of her fears Mildred Doran said "I'm going," dried her tears, climbed aboard the plane, and settled down for a long ride. But the initial thrill was gone. Those who were closest to her when she boarded the plane commented that she wasn't her usual smiling self, and, as later events unfolded, possibly she had a woman's intuition of impending doom.

Finally at 2:03 P.M., almost two hours behind the leaders, the *Miss Doran* again started down the runway, lifted off, and slowly climbed across the bay through the Golden Gate and out over the Pacific.

By this time most of the planes that had escorted the entrants out past the Golden Gate were returning. Billy Parker had escorted Art Goebel to the Farallone Islands before waving good-bye. He reported the fog bank still extended past the Farallones, but otherwise the weather looked good.

After about an hour the crowd concluded the party was over and began to disperse. It looked like a race was on. Two planes, *El Encanto* and *Pabco Pacific Flyer*, lay wrecked on the field. Three more, *City of Peoria*, *Oklahoma*, and *Dallas Spirit* were parked back at the starting area. Four more, *Woolaroc*, *Aloha*, *Miss Doran*, and *Golden Eagle*, were somewhere over the lonely Pacific.

After it was certain that only four planes would be in the race that night, the Radio Corporation of America sent the following message to all ships in the Pacific:

> Airplanes passing over ships tonight will signal their starting number with a pocket flashlight. Number 4 Golden Eagle will give four flashes. Number 5 Miss Doran will give five flashes. Number 7 Aloha seven flashes. Number 8 Woolaroc eight flashes. Please keep close watch and report position and passing. Woolaroc KGGI equipped with 100 watt transmitter 600 meters. Golden Eagle equipped with receiver only call KWS.

As happens whenever man attempts to conquer a new and unknown adversary, the whole world waited—and prayed.

10

ACROSS THE PACIFIC

Four planes, carrying eight men and a girl, were finally on their way. Of the four, only the *Woolaroc* was equipped with a radio transmitter. The *Golden Eagle* had a receiver, while the *Miss Doran* and *Aloha* had neither.

First reports started coming in before the last of the contestants had left the ground. At 1:05 P.M. the Navy station in the Farallone Islands reported the *Aloha* had passed over at an altitude of 50 feet. Marty Jensen was flying low exactly as he had planned, giving Paul Schluter every opportunity to obtain a good reading on the horizon.

At 2:00 P.M. the motorship *Silver Fir*, off the California coast, picked up radio signals from the *Woolaroc* and at 2:35 P.M. reporting sighting the *Aloha* as it passed overhead at a very low altitude. The report gave the position as latitude 37.18° and longitude 125.04° or approximately 185 miles out of San Francisco. Weather conditions were improving with a slight northwest wind, moderate seas, and a slight haze. This report was somewhat optimistic as the position reported would indicate the *Aloha* was making a ground speed of 92 miles per hour. Without a helpful tailwind this was too high for the Breese monoplane at this stage of the flight. Most of the planes were expected to average 75 to 85 miles per hour, gradually increasing their speed to about 95 miles per hour as their fuel was burned off. Probably the navigator on the *Silver Fir* roughly estimated his position. With the fog conditions it would be very easy to err by 10 or 15 miles.

At 2:45 P.M. the Navy station in the Farallones reported an unidentified plane, believed to be the *Miss Doran*, passed over the base. By now reports were coming in at regular intervals. By 2:50 P.M the S. S. *Wilhelmina* reported sighting the *Aloha* slightly north of their position at latitude 36.57° and longitude 125.01° or approximately 175 miles from San Francisco. Jensen and Schluter, having been airborne 2 hours 16 minutes, were making good a ground speed of more than 77 miles per hour.

A 3:03 P.M. report from the Farallones told of sighting the *Miss Doran* passing out of sight in a westerly direction and still climbing. At 4:00 P.M. one of the naval vessels reported the *Aloha* 35 miles north of the great circle route approximately on course. At the same time the *Wilhelmina* picked up the *Woolaroc* reporting a position about 263 miles west of San Francisco. Bill Davis reported the radio signals were "coming in fine." The *Wilhelmina* continued to maintain contact with the *Woolaroc* until 4:35 P.M. At that time they reported Davis and Goebel in good condition and relayed a message from Davis to his parents.

Up to this time, probably due to the hazy conditions, only two of the aircraft had been sighted and positively identified. The *Aloha* sightings were due to the very low altitude that Jensen was holding and the huge name painted on both sides of the fuselage, readable at a great distance. The *Miss Doran* was readily identified as it was the only biplane in the race.

At 5:30 P.M. the first of many false reports came in, this one from one of the Navy destroyers. They reported sighting the *Aloha* 250 miles from San Francisco and estimated its speed at 84 miles per hour. After flying nearly five hours the *Aloha* would have averaged only 50 miles per hour to be at that point. If they really spotted a plane it was probably the *Miss Doran*, which would have averaged 72 miles per hour to be at that point.

At 8:00 P.M. Pacific time a report was picked up from the *Woolaroc* stating they were 604 miles west of Oakland on course. Davis added, "Seven hours out and all going fine." He again sent a separate message to his worried parents. From this it was estimated that *Woolaroc* was averaging 82 miles per hour.

Another 8:00 P.M. report from the destroyer *McDonough* showed the *Woolaroc* 517 miles west of San Francisco, which at first glance appears erroneous. However, this probably was 517 nautical miles, or 595 statute miles. This confirms the previous report and a cruising speed of 81 to 83 miles per hour. A third 8:00 P.M. report by the Army Signal Corps listed the *Woolaroc* 550 miles from San Francisco at 63 miles per hour. This was obviously false.

At 8:30 P.M. the U.S.S. *Corey* reported the *Woolaroc* was approaching their position at 640 miles from San Francisco. Twenty minutes later they reported a new position of 687 miles. Both of these reports indicated a respectable 81 to 83 miles per hour cruising speed.

For the next few hours there was silence. Then another series of conflicting and false reports were received. At 11:07 P.M. the S.S. *President Harrison* reported from midocean that "planes" were estimated to pass over the ship in two hours. As only one plane had a transmitter they could not have received word from "planes."

At 11:00 P.M. the *Corey* reported the *Woolaroc* as 700 miles from San Francisco at an estimated speed of 86.9 miles per hour. It would have been closer to 65 miles per hour if the report were true. At 11:30 P.M. the Signal Corps erred again: this time they reported Goebel had passed through an area of high winds and had averaged 63 miles per hour, but between 11:00 and 11:30 P.M. he averaged 120 miles per hour. Remarkable if true.

At midnight the Signal Corps reported Goebel 950 to 1,000 miles from San Francisco and 12 hours from Hawaii. At 1:00 A.M. they updated their report and estimated Goebel's speed at 120 miles per hour with arrival between 10:00 A.M. and noon Honolulu time.

About this time a report was released at Oakland that Frost and Scott were leading the pack. There was no basis for the report, but the crowds around the newspaper offices were elated.

At 2:00 A.M. Pacific time the S.S. *City of Los Angeles* reported sighting a plane, tentatively identified as the *Golden Eagle*, midway across the ocean. Based on the 12:31 P.M. takeoff time of the *Golden Eagle*, in thirteen and a half hours it should have been well past halfway. The plane seen was probably the *Aloha* as it was flying low and would have been about halfway at that time. Another report came in at 2:00 A.M.—this one from the S.S. *Manulani* at 31.45° north latitude and 139.30° west longitude or 1,425 miles from Honolulu. Two planes had been sighted within a few minutes of one another, and they received the call letters KGGI from one. This, of course, was the *Woolaroc*. No contact was made with the other. The *Manulani*'s report indicated that both planes were averaging about 75 miles per hour. The report was confirmed by another from the S.S. *Mani* at about 2:15 A.M. Pacific time. Two unidentified planes flew over their position at 1,132 miles from the nearest Hawaiian point. They probably used nautical miles, which would convert to about 1,300 miles.

It is interesting to speculate on the relative positions of the *Woolaroc* and the *Aloha* during their flights. Assuming the 2:50 P.M. reports from the S.S. *Wilhelmina* were correct, the *Aloha* had covered 175 miles in 2 hours and 16 minutes, averaging 77.2 miles per hour, 1.287 miles per minute. The 4:00 P.M. report indicates the *Woolaroc* had covered 263 miles in 3 hours and 24 minutes for an average speed of 77.35 miles per hour or 1.289 miles per minute. The *Woolaroc* started two minutes or 2.57 miles behind the *Aloha*. With their relative speeds so close to each other the *Woolaroc* would only gain 0.15 mph or about 800 feet per hour on the *Aloha*. To catch up 2 ½ miles would take roughly 17 hours. Actually both planes slowly improved their cruising speeds as they burned off fuel and lightened their loads. Using fuel at about 12 to 13 gallons per hour would decrease the weight by about 75 to 85 pounds per hour. The actual throttle setting, altitude flown, and deviations from a true course would all influence their relative positions. The anticipated improvement in cruising speed was very evident by the speeds later reported by the *Woolaroc* as 86 to 87 miles per hour.

Later developments would show it was almost certain that the two planes crossing the S.S. *Manulani* at midocean during the night were the *Woolaroc* and the *Aloha*. Yet neither crew saw the other; apparently they were truly "ships that pass in the night."

Throughout the long evening hours there were some authentic reports, but all of them concerned the *Woolaroc*, the *Aloha*, or the *Miss Doran*. All three of these crews were flying the race as predicted by Billy Parker. He had recommended to Goebel to climb above the fog at the start. Art climbed to about 1,500 feet over San Francisco and continued to climb until he was above the clouds shortly after passing the Golden Gate. He later reported he flew as high as 6,000 feet. Jack Frost, in the *Golden Eagle*, though he did not have the benefit of Billy Parker's advice, chose to fly above the fog from the start. He did have the advantage of the best-performing airplane and was easily able to climb through the overcast shortly after leaving Oakland. Lee Schoenhair, a prominent Army flier, followed the *Golden Eagle* for about 115 miles out over the Pacific before waving good-bye. He reported that Frost had climbed to 2,000 feet, where he found clear air above the cloud bank just as Parker had predicted.

Newspapers on the mainland and in Honolulu had set up special listening posts to accumulate all reports and distribute them to the public. This was good planning before the race when it was expected that six of the planes would be using radio transmitters. By coincidence, only one plane with a transmitter started across the Pacific. Reports could be received only from Goebel and Davis, and they did not transmit very often. After the first few hours time passed slowly for the anxious listeners on shore.

Then the reports started to come from the Hawaiian stations or ships close to Hawaii. Times were reported in Honolulu time, two and a half hours earlier than Pacific time.

At about midnight in Honolulu many people started the 25-mile drive from the city to Wheeler Field. An endless line of head lights pointed the way to the field. Rain squalls started about the same time, turning into heavy rain about 1:30 in the morning. Field kitchens were set up by the Army, and many of the early arrivals slept in their cars after finding a good parking space. Mrs. Jensen arrived at the field about 2:00 A.M. and, undaunted by the rain, told reporters, "I'm confident Martin will be the first to arrive." A short while later the rain stopped and the heavy clouds started to lift. Meanwhile, the first reports directly from Goebel were starting to filter into Honolulu. At 1:30 A.M. Honolulu time, Goebel reported passing a ship about 1,000 miles from Honolulu and guessed it was the S.S. *President Harrison*, but apparently he was mistaken. He reported tailwinds of 13 to 15 miles per hour. His speed was increasing due to these favorable winds, and he now was averaging about 90 miles per hour.

At 3:30 A.M. the S.S. *City of Los Angeles* at 825 miles from Honolulu reported that Goebel was 100 miles ahead of the ship, or 725 miles from the finish line. This position would indicate about a 96-mile-per-hour average and was somewhat optimistic. Another report about the same time from the S.S. *President Harrison*, 700 miles from Honolulu, confirmed that Goebel was in the vicinity but could not pinpoint his position.

The Army Signal Corps rejoined the act reporting Goebel averaging 83 miles per hour and estimating his arrival at 1:30 P.M. in Honolulu. To add to the confusion the Mutual Telephone Company reported Goebel as 400 miles from Honolulu, and a private radio club in Honolulu reported him as 800 miles away. All these reports were made within a few minutes of each other. At 3:55 A.M. the Army station at Wheeler Field added to the confusion by announcing that no reports had been received for the past few hours.

As dawn approached more and more people were arriving at Wheeler Field. Reports continued to be confusing, and no one really knew how many fliers were still in the air or where any of them actually were. Far out over the Pacific at least two planes were droning steadily westward with four apprehensive and extremely tired fliers looking forward to dawn.

On board the *Aloha* things were going as expected. Earlier, as night fell, Marty Jensen decided he had better climb over the fog, which was still hanging over the ocean even though they had traveled almost 1,000 miles. He planned to climb high enough to enable Paul Schluter to obtain a positive fix on the stars. Also he knew there was an almost full moon shining above the clouds, which would provide a lighted horizon for reference and would help build up the fliers' morale. Things always go better when you can see where you are going. He assumed the fog bank was a few hundred feet thick and started to climb through it, relying on his past, limited experience at blind flying. At about 4,000 feet Jensen experienced what today is termed vertigo. At the time all he knew was that he lost control of the *Aloha* and started to spin. After recovering he again tried to climb. After two more spins he realized he couldn't get above the fog, so he dropped down close to the ocean surface.

Jensen was flying extremely low—he estimated it as about 10 feet— when he tried to hand his flashlight to Schluter and accidently leaned forward on the stick. He felt a sharp bump as one of the wheels hit a wave. Instinctively he pulled up and managed to keep flying. Later he found a foot long rip in the fuselage fabric that probably was a result of the bump. Marty decided to remain below the clouds, but from there on he flew at 100 to 200 feet, even though this meant ducking in and out of the bottom of the fog bank. Though there was a nearly full moon high in the sky, below the clouds there was only a faint glow, which gave little indication of a horizon. Schluter could not take any readings on the stars, and Jensen had considerable difficulty throughout the night maintaining the *Aloha* in a normal level attitude. There never was an opportunity throughout the night to check the wind drift. The longer they flew the more Jensen and Schluter realized they would be very lucky even to find Hawaii, let alone win the race.

Compared to the *Aloha*, the *Woolaroc* was having a routine flight. Art Goebel broke through the clouds at about 2,000 feet shortly after he left Oakland. In the bright sunshine he headed west for Honolulu. The trusty Wright J-5 performed perfectly throughout the day, and Goebel continued to stay above the clouds. As evening approached the cloud tops rose and he had to keep climbing to stay above them. He finally leveled off at about 6,000 feet to remain in the clear. Their radio direction finder was the same one used by Smith and Bronte in June. It worked well and provided Goebel with good signals most of the way.

At one time during the night both Goebel and Davis had quite a scare. Davis had crawled back through the fuselage to check the earth inductor compass. This instrument consists of three parts, a generator, a controller, and an indicator. The generator part was mounted behind the cabin area on top of the fuselage with a wind-driven vane outside and the actual generator inside. The generator could be serviced, if necessary, in flight from within the fuselage. The brushes of the generaator frequently required changing during a long flight, and a spare set was attached to the generator cover. Bill had removed the spares and put them in his pocket. As he was oiling the bearings the spare set of brushes slipped from his pocket and slid under the floor boards onto the fabric bottom of the fuselage. The brushes lying on the vibrating fabric produced a noise that was almost the same as the sound of a burned-out valve in an engine. Both Davis and Goebel were afraid they were about to experience an engine failure. Davis started to prepare their life raft, removed his shoes, and got ready to make a hasty exit. But the trusty engine continued to purr. After a short time Davis realized the noise wasn't coming from the engine, and he started to look for the source. When he discovered the brushes causing the noise he breathed a sigh of relief and, as he said later, "threw them out of the plane as far as I could."

Goebel and Davis continued to fly steadily toward Hawaii throughout the night without further problems. They ate almost all their sandwiches, drank their milk and coffee, and waited for the dawn. The pulley arrangement for transferring notes broke down during the night, and they were unable to communicate very well because of the noise of the engine, but otherwise the trip was smooth. Their only problem was to keep from falling asleep as the monotonous drone of the engine went on hour after hour.

We can only speculate what happened on board the *Miss Doran*. We know Augy Pedlar originally took off at 12:33 P.M. and had to return about 1:00 P.M. After completing repairs on his engine, and knowing only three other aircraft were actually in the race, Pedlar took off again at 2:03 P.M. This time they were successful, and they crossed the Farallone Islands at 2:45 P.M. By three o'clock they had their last look at land as the Farallones dropped below the horizon. The engine was running smoothly at this point, exactly one hour after takeoff. One of the numerous circling planes reported they were making good progress and certainly weren't experiencing any of their previous troubles.

Augy Pedlar, pilot, brash, young, and sometimes overly vocal, was starting on the most dangerous and longest flight of his life. Lt. Vilas Knope, navigator, had just been able to obtain leave from his naval duties on Saturday, 13 August, to accompany his friend on the flight. M. A. Lawing, Pedlar's original choice, had failed the navigator's test and agreed to step down, and, as later events unfolded, he must have thanked his lucky stars for that decision. Knope, being a qualified navigator, was probably the only one of the three that fully realized the seriousness of the flight. Mildred Doran was still a schoolgirl at heart, tremendously thrilled at the prospect of flying the Pacific and little appreciating the vast expanse of water to be crossed or the risks involved.

To reconstruct the events of the next few hours requires some imagination. The *Miss Doran*, being the only biplane in the race as well as the most brightly colored plane, should have been easy to identify if it passed near any of the ships at sea. Also with the heavy fuel load of 400 gallons, three crew members, and special cabin equipment for Mildred Doran, Pedlar almost assuredly chose to stay below the overcast rather than risk losing control or overheating the engine by climbing up through the fog.

Four times in the first few hours of flight the *Aloha*, also flying low and easy to identify, was spotted by people on the ground or at sea. It seems, in the comparatively heavily traveled sea lanes off shore of San Francisco, someone would have spotted the *Miss Doran* if it remained in the air for many hours. After the first hour of flight only one report that could have been the *Miss Doran* was received. This was from a Navy destroyer that reported sighting a plane at 5:30 P.M. 250 miles from San Francisco. They falsely identified it as the *Aloha*, but it probably was the *Miss Doran*. Past this point it is anyone's guess.

A possible scenario follows. The engine probably started again to run rough. In a last desperate effort to save the plane and crew Augy Pedlar turned back toward land and prayed the engine would hold out. By this time, four or five hours after takeoff, the *Miss Doran* had probably climbed above the fog. In order to have the best chance of being spotted or to see any passing ships, Pedlar probably started to glide back through the clouds. Either the engine quit or Pedlar became disoriented, lost control of the heavily loaded Buhl in the glide, and started to spin toward the ocean only a few hundred feet below. Things can happen awfully fast, and he probably didn't have time to dump the fuel from the main tanks. When he saw the ocean it was already too late. He must have tried to level off but was unsuccessful. Few airplanes can withstand even a gentle crash at sea; most will sink within a minute or two. The end must have been quick—no chance to launch a raft—the entire plane and its crew probably sank immediately. If there had been time to jettison the fuel, the empty tanks would have kept the plane afloat for many hours, but this was not to be. No debris was ever found, no flares were ever seen, no trace was left that the *Miss Doran* had ever existed.

The flight of the *Golden Eagle* is a little harder to reconstruct. At 12:30 P.M. Jack Frost and Gordon Scott made the best takeoff of any of the contestants. They headed west, past downtown San Francisco, climbing steadily in order to get into the clear skies above the clouds. Lee Schoenhair flew with them for more than 100 miles and waved goodbye at about 2,000 feet over the Pacific in bright sunlight. At this point the *Golden Eagle* was performing faultlessly and appeared to be leading the pack. It should have been a smooth flight to Hawaii.

Maybe it is wishful thinking, but I believe the *Golden Eagle* reached Hawaii. I believe Jack Frost remained above the clouds all the way, climbing to 6,000 or 7,000 feet to remain on top during the night. I also believe they made better time than they anticipated, averaging more than 100 miles per hour. As the first traces of dawn appeared over the Pacific I believe the *Golden Eagle* was far ahead of the *Woolaroc* and the *Aloha* and much closer to Hawaii than either Gordon Scott or Jack Frost realized.

The clouds were still hanging on at dawn with the *Woolaroc* and *Golden Eagle* above them and the *Aloha* below. I believe the *Golden Eagle* was leading by far with the *Aloha* second and the *Woolaroc* a close third. All three were coming out of the last turn and heading into the home stretch for the race to the wire.

11

THE FINISH

When the first faint traces of dawn appeared over the Pacific on 17 August, it was a welcome sight to at least four fliers. Art Goebel and Bill Davis had been flying the *Woolaroc* at an altitude of about 6,000 feet all night without so much as a glimpse of water. They were tired, cold, worried, and irritable. Having taken off in seventh place and knowing the *El Encanto* had crashed on takeoff and the *Pabco Pacific Flyer* had not gotten off the ground, Goebel and Davis were sure that four planes were ahead of them. They were also reasonably sure that the *Dallas Spirit* was following close behind them. They knew the *Aloha* was slightly faster and the *Golden Eagle* was much faster than their plane. Their sister ship, the *Oklahoma*, should perform the same as the *Woolaroc*, but it had a 36-minute advantage due to its number one takeoff position. Goebel and Davis had resigned themselves to their primary job of reaching Hawaii safely, and both assumed they would not win.

At 4:30 A.M. Honolulu time, Davis radioed the *Woolaroc*'s position as 650 miles from Honolulu. After the sun rose and they were better able to determine their position, Davis sent a location message of 24.35° north latitude 150.43° west longitude or 450 miles from Honolulu.

Shortly after dawn the morning edition of the Honolulu *Advertiser* reported that Martin Jensen in the *Aloha* was leading the race and that Davis sent a message to his wife. They were wrong on both counts: by that time Jensen was 200 miles off course, and Davis wasn't married.

Since passing over the Farallones neither Goebel nor Davis had seen any other plane. Even after the sun rose they were still above the clouds and the sky was empty from horizon to horizon. About 9:00 A.M. they had a brief glimpse of the water but only for a few minutes. Davis reported they were nearing Oahu, and at 9:40 A.M. he followed up with a position report, 22° north latitude 154.30° west longitude, heading for Maui, 120 miles out and 200 miles from Honolulu. Between ten and eleven o'clock they saw the water, but this time land was on the horizon to their left, Goebel was sure it was Maui. A few minutes later he sighted Molokai to their right and headed toward it. In Honolulu the Naval Station had been closely monitoring the radio reports, and at 10:30 A.M. four patrol planes commanded by Cmdr. M. B. McComb took off to meet the fliers. Army pilots were in the air over Wheeler Field, each hoping to be the first to spot the winner. At this stage Goebel and Davis were almost delirious with joy. Due to their inability to communicate with each other, except with crude hand signs, Davis misinterpreted one of Goebel's signals and thought they were running out of fuel. Goebel pointed the *Woolaroc* directly across the channel between Molokai and Oahu and started pointing toward Honolulu. Davis thought he was asking if they should try to make it or land at Molokai. Davis signaled to go ahead, figuring they were close enough to glide or swim if the engine quit. He started firing his Very Flare pistol and dropping smoke bombs until they were past Diamond Head and almost within sight of Wheeler Field. Army planes, circling in the vicinity, saw the *Woolaroc* in the distance and started to escort it to a landing. Goebel was sure some of the other contestants had already arrived and made no effort to rush to a landing. Finally one of the Army pilots, in a PW-9 pursuit plane, was able to get close enough to hold up his hand and signal number one. Suddenly Goebel realized what the Army pilot was trying to tell him—he could still win—so he quickly landed and taxied up in front of the crowded stands. At 12:24 P.M. Honolulu time the *Woolaroc* officially touched down to capture first place in the Pacific Air Race. Art Goebel and Bill Davis were greeted by thousands of wildly cheering spectators.

As Davis jumped out of the plane his first words were "How are the rest of the boys?" When informed that nothing had been heard from any of the others, both Goebel and Davis lost much of their enthusiasm.

Their landing time, 12:24 P.M. in Hawaii, was 2:54 P.M. Pacific time in Oakland because of a two and a half hour difference between the mainland and the islands. Total time for the flight was 26 hours 19 minutes 33 seconds. One of the first spectators to reach the side of the *Woolaroc*, when it stopped rolling, was Peg Jensen. Upon being informed by Art Goebel that they hadn't seen any of the other fliers she temporarily collapsed beside the plane. In a few minutes she regained composure and tried to convince herself the *Aloha* would be arriving soon.

The crowd repeatedly cheered Goebel and Davis as they slowly made their way to the receiving stand. When they were finally able to climb up on the stand they were officially welcomed by some of the dignitaries, and both pilot and navigator expressed their joy and surprise at being the first to arrive. The remarks were tempered by the somber thoughts that at least one of the others should have arrived before them, but aloud each assured the crowd that more of the boys would soon arrive. They were driven into town to the Royal Hawaiian Hotel. Though they were both physically tired, they were also keyed up to the point where they had to unwind for a few hours before they would be able to rest. At the hotel they were again besieged by crowds of well-wishers in the lobby, each intent on personally talking to the fliers and taking their pictures. After a short time they were ushered to their suite where the press continued to interview them. Goebel insisted he wanted a shave and haircut, and Davis agreed to a shave. While the barber was working a huge buffet luncheon was brought to their rooms. Included were fried chicken, alligator pears, tomatoes, and a good supply of local Hawaiian fruits. Davis was quite hungry, but Goebel said he was not. While Davis was eating and Goebel was preparing for a swim, the telephone rang and they were informed that Marty Jensen and Paul Schluter had just landed at Wheeler Field. "That's wonderful news," Davis said. "I'm certainly glad that he made it," was Goebel's comment, "and all we hope is that the others come through safely." Later in the afternoon both fliers relaxed with a swim at famed Waikiki Beach. Shortly after that they both retired for a well-earned rest.

Earlier that morning of 17 August, Marty Jensen and Paul Schluter had still been flying below the overcast a scant 100 feet above the water. They were most anxious for daylight in order to take celestial observations to confirm their position. Having flown for about 20 hours without any opportunity to obtain a sighting on any stars or even a good check on wind drift they were naturally worried that they might be off course. Jensen had flown the entire distance with one hand on the throttle and the other on the stick. His only respite had come during the periods when he had to use the hand wobble pump to transfer fuel from the fuselage tank to the wing tanks. Every muscle ached, and he strained to catch the first hint of dawn. At least daylight would make it a little easier to maintain the *Aloha* straight and level. But the coming of dawn was scarcely any improvement. The overcast still prevailed, so they had little choice but to continue westward. At about 9:30 A.M. Honolulu time, after some 24 hours of flying Jensen felt they should have sighted land. Some of the ground spotters agreed with him, because at about 11:00 the *Aloha* was reported at Hilo and again about 11:30 between Pearl Harbor and Honolulu. The number of Army and Navy planes flying in the vicinity caused many premature reports throughout the morning.

Now it was daylight, and visibility had improved somewhat, but Schluter felt he could not obtain an accurate sight of the sun until it reached its maximum point at noon, which was still two and a half hours away. He told Jensen to circle for the two and a half hours, which did little to improve the pilot's opinion of his navigator. Jensen cut the engine back as far as he could to conserve fuel. At this time Schluter looked inside the fuel tank and, seeing an exposed baffle plate, assumed the tank was empty. He told Jensen of his findings, and, though Jensen could not believe they were that close to empty, he knew they were not far from it. Schluter's information meant that they had only what fuel remained in the wing tanks, which was not enough to last for two and a half hours. Jensen tried to pump every last drop from the fuselage tank into the wing tanks. He passed the next few hours on pins and needles because of what later proved to be Schluter's erroneous assumption.

At noon Jensen maintained a 100-foot altitude while Schluter took a series of readings showing they were almost exactly 200 miles north of Oahu. Jensen changed course to due south and periodically continued to pump more fuel into the wing tanks, expecting to run dry at any moment. His anxiety was heightened by the lack of fuel gauges on the wing tanks. The only way he knew his wing tanks were full was when the fuel spilled out the overflow drains while he was pumping. This added to the problem because a small amount of fuel was lost each time the upper tanks were filled, and at the same time the overflowing fuel created a fire hazard. After flying for two hours due south, Jensen changed to a 235° compass heading and in a few minutes sighted land. He recognized Oahu, crossed the low-lying mountains, and headed straight for Wheeler Field. As they prepared to land they could see one plane parked in front of the hanger but could not tell which one it was. By this time Jensen and Schluter had given up all hope of coming in first or second—all they wanted to do was get down safely and get some rest. Jensen wondered how many planes were inside the hanger, probably so many had arrived that they had no room for the one parked outside. Anyway the stands were still filled so they must be still expecting the *Aloha*. Jensen, ever the showman, deciding he might as well make it look good for the crowd, swung gracefully into the wind and made a beautiful landing. He taxied up past the other plane, which he now recognized as the *Woolaroc*, and rolled to a stop at the center of the stands. It was 2:20 P.M. local time or 4:50 P.M. back in Oakland. Total time for the flight was 28 hours 16 minutes. It had been a long day.

The *Aloha* was immediately surrounded by a joyous crowd. Jensen's wife rushed out to the plane and loudly shouted "Marty Jensen—where the hell have you been?" But all Jensen recalled of those hectic moments was seeing Hawaiian Governor Farrington climb up to the *Aloha*'s cockpit and eat one of the leftover sandwiches. Both Jensen and Schluter had to be repeatedly told that they had won the second place before they really believed it. Both felt that, after losing two and a half hours aimlessly circling a deserted spot in the Pacific Ocean, they would be last. In truth they were. Or as Jensen liked to describe the finish of the Dole race, "I came in next to first place and Goebel came in next to last." Only two planes of the original group of fifteen that were assigned starting positions made it to Hawaii. From their takeoff to their landing Jensen and Schluter never caught sight of any of the other planes, and without radio equipment they had no way of knowing of the progress of the other contestants. After being told that Art Goebel and Bill Davis in the *Woolaroc* had landed at 12:24 P.M. Jensen did some quick figuring and realized he would have been more than 30 minutes ahead of Goebel if Schluter had been able to obtain an accurate sight without insisting on circling for two and a half hours.

After the initial hectic greeting came a series of short speeches and congratulations from the assembled dignitaries. Jensen and Schluter were both concerned about the other fliers. They were very surprised that only four planes had actually started for Honolulu. The two planes still unaccounted for were both reliable and well proven in Jensen's opinion, and both he and Schluter assured the crowd they should be arriving any time.

As evening came on, most of the crowd realized that no more planes would be arriving. Most estimates were in agreement that the *Golden Eagle* was out of fuel by three or four o'clock and the *Miss Doran* ran out about 8:30 P.M.

At sunset a mass exodus started away from the field. Long lines of cars headed back to Honolulu. Marty Jensen and his wife, Peg, together with Paul Schluter, were driven to the Royal Hawaiian Hotel, where they retired for the night.

Both the *Woolaroc* and the *Aloha* suffered some damage from the souvenir seekers, in spite of the valiant efforts of the police and military personnel to protect them. As most of the crowd left, the two planes were pushed into the hanger for further protection and examination. The remaining fuel was drained from both planes and measured to determine how much longer each could have remained aloft. The *Woolaroc* had approximately 50 gallons, or enough for three to four hours flying time. The *Aloha* had about four gallons, which would have allowed about 20 more minutes of flight.

The following morning the reporters interviewed all four fliers and took many pictures at the Royal Hawaiian Hotel. They were questioned on every aspect of their flights. One of the reporters asked Marty Jensen and Paul Schluter to demonstrate their life raft by riding in it a short distance from shore. They followed the instructions on the raft, but try as they would it would not inflate. Finally, in order to get the picture, they inflated it with a tire pump and paddled out from the shore for the picture.

In the afternoon a formal presentation was held on the patio of the Royal Hawaiian Hotel. James Dole presented a check for 25,000 dollars to

Art Goebel and one for 10,000 dollars to Marty Jensen. These were special checks hand-painted with pictures of an airplane and the islands. After cashing and perforating them with the date, the bank returned them to Goebel and Jensen as souvenirs. The presentation ceremonies were brief, out of respect for the fliers who were still missing. Both pilots made short acceptance speeches and expressed their joy at being there, but there was a sense of gloom over the festivities. Hope was expressed by all the speakers that the missing fliers would still be found but Goebel and Jensen, more than any of the others, knew in their hearts there was little chance. They knew exactly how big the Pacific was and how empty it could be.

12

MEANWHILE, BACK AT THE FIELD

Hardly had Art Goebel and Marty Jensen landed at Honolulu when the owners of the *City of Peoria* filed a formal protest with the Department of Commerce over the last- minute disqualification of their Air King biplane. It had been officially disqualified at about 11:15 A.M., just before the noon start of the race on Tuesday, 16 August, based on a lack of sufficient fuel as defined in the race rules. The owners had been repeatedly warned of the possibility of disqualification and as late as Monday, 15 August, they were told if they would add an additional fuel tank the committee would qualify the airplane.

Various charges involving passing the buck and subterfuge were thrown back and forth by Parkhurst and Lowes. Bernard Kelley, attorney, acting for the National Airways System, owners of the plane, told the press that the action by the race committee was nonsense. Both he and S. F. Tannus said they were in the dark as to the real reason for the disqualification. "We knew nothing about our disqualification until 11:00 oclock that morning, just one hour before the race." This was not entirely true because the early morning issues of the San Francisco papers had carried stories concerning the *City of Peoria*. One article discussed whether it could meet the fuel-capacity requirements. Another mentioned that at 9:00 A.M. the plane had been moved up to the starting line after the officials had held an early morning conference. The conclusion, naturally, was that the differences had been resolved and the *City of Peoria* would be allowed to start.

Apparently the plane had originally passed its required tests on Saturday, 13 August. Art Starbuck, test pilot, had flown the *City of Peoria* and reported it cruised at 99 miles per hour and the fuel consumption was approximately 12 gallons per hour. These tests were performed with a 50 percent fuel load and served only as a general indication of the capabilities of the plane.

The committee had already decided to use 13 gallons per hour as the standard fuel consumption for Wright J–5 engines. At 99 miles per hour cruising speed and 368 gallons of fuel the *City of Peoria* should have just barely made it under the wire with about a 16 to 17 percent reserve. But Charlie Parkhurst and Ralph Lowes both knew that 99 miles per hour was a very optimistic speed.

A few days earlier, on 11 August, Parkhurst and Lowes had arrived at Oakland in a tired and worn *City of Peoria*. They had a rough trip and were ready to give up. A quick review of their trip shows how right they were. Following is the log of the *City of Peoria* as near as it can be constructed from available data, starting with the roll-out from the factory:

Date		Flight	Time/Distance	Speed
Aug. 8	A.M.	10 min. test	—	—
	7:00 P.M.	Take-off Carman, Ill.	Est. 230 miles	—
	9:30 P.M.	Land, Ottumwa, Iowa	2 1/2 hours	92 mph.
Aug. 9	5:53 A.M.	Take-off Ottumwa, Iowa	180 miles	
	7:50 A.M.	Land Omaha, Neb.	1 hr. 57 min.	92 mph.
	10:00 A.M.	Take-off Omaha, Neb.	490 miles	
	Evening	Land Cheyenne, Wyo.	—	—
Aug. 10	6:50 A.M.	Take-off Cheyenne, Wyo.	440 miles	
	1:30 P.M.	Land, Salt Lake City, Utah	6 hrs. 40 min.	66 mph.
Aug. 11		Take-off Salt Lake City	220 miles	
		Land Elko, Nev.	3 hrs. 7 min.	60 mph.
		Take-off Elko, Nev.	280 miles	
		Land Reno, Nev.	3 hrs. 20 min.	84 mph.
		Take-off Reno, Nev.	190 miles	
		Land Oakland, Calif.	2 hrs. 45 min.	69 mph.

The log isn't exactly impressive, as the only reasonably good cruising speed was 92 miles per hour and that was maintained only for approximately four hours.

In fairness to the backers of the *City of Peoria* it must be admitted that the speeds recorded were ground speeds. No record was made of the headwinds that were encountered. As the prevailing winds are usually from the west they were probably bucking some wind, at least from Cheyenne to Oakland, and the actual cruising speed attained was probably close to 90 miles per hour.

On Friday, 12 August, the crew repaired their damaged plane. By Saturday they had it ready to fly, and it was checked out by the committee. Though there was serious doubt about the fuel capacity and suggestions were made that an additional tank should be added, the committee tentatively approved the plane. Parkhurst and Lowes were concerned about their own tests, but on Sunday Parkhurst passed the pilot's test, and they both qualified as navigators.

On Monday, 15 August, Parkhurst apparently decided the plane would never make the 2,400 mile flight. But he and Lowes still had a contract with S. F. Tannus, and opinions weren't included in the contract. Parkhurst voiced his opinion to the officials stating that he did not think the cruising speed would be much more than 80 miles per hour. At that speed they would run out of fuel about 150 miles short of Honolulu. Naturally his complaint created a storm of controversy. When S. F. Tannus heard about it he was infuriated and immediately fired the crew and had the name "City of Peoria" removed from both sides of the plane's engine cowling. Neither Parkhurst nor Lowes seemed to be too upset about losing their jobs, in fact they appeared to be relieved. Tannus did leave their names on both sides of the cockpit, together with other identifying marks and names. He tried to recruit a new crew, and his right hand man, Edward Lagron, said he would be willing to take the job of pilot. Reports are very sketchy, but at this point apparently Art Starbuck again flew the airplane and now reported the Air King incapable of maintaining more than 90 miles per hour cruising speed. Though the committee still did not officially disqualify the plane, it was obvious that, if the assigned crew did not have faith in their plane, the committee was not going to approve it.

The big day, Tuesday, 16 August, arrived, and at an early hour all the entrants were moved up to the starting circle. This action prompted the rumor that the *City of Peoria* would be allowed to start. But the crew members were still reluctant to fly. Lagron again stated he would fly the plane, but the committee refused to allow any substitutions at that late hour. Finally the race committee took the bull by the horns and at 11:15 A.M. handed Charlie Parkhurst the official notice disqualifying the *City of Peoria*. It read "We consider this plane has insufficient gasoline capacity for the required mileage" and was signed by Walter F. Barkin and C. W. Breinger, Department of Commerce airplane inspectors.

Now comes further confusion in the saga of the *City of Peoria*. S. F. Tannus, Charlie Parkhurst, and Ralph Lowes made a lot of noise but did not take any formal action. However Tannus did voice his opinion to the press and strongly hinted he was planning legal action. After the *Golden Eagle* was reported missing on Thursday some of the Air King group tried to create the impression that it had been permitted to take off with less gasoline than the rules allowed. Later in the day a formal protest was wired to William McCracken, assistant secretary of commerce in charge of aviation.

WILL YOU PLEASE INAUGURATE AN INVESTIGATION AS TO WHY THE GOLDEN EAGLE NOW MISSING WAS PERMITTED TO LEAVE

AIRPORT CARRYING ONLY 350 GALLONS OF GASOLINE. YOUR REPRESENTATIVE HERE SAYS ALL SHIPS FIGURED ON BASIS OF 13 GALLONS PER HOUR GAS CONSUMPTION IN CRUISING SPEED OF 90 MPH IT WAS UPON THIS BASIS THAT OUR ENTRY CITY OF PEORIA WAS DISQUALIFIED CARRYING 18 GALLONS MORE THAN THE GOLDEN EAGLE. UNDER THE RULES OF FIFTEEN PERCENT SURPLUS SAFETY MARGIN THE GOLDEN EAGLE SHOULD HAVE CARRIED 397 GALLONS OF GAS THEY LEFT WITH 350 WHICH IS 47 GALLONS SHY OF REGULATIONS. SIGNED BERNARD KELLEY ATTORNEY NATIONAL AIRWAYS SYSTEM CAPTAIN EDWARD LAGRON BUSINESS MANAGER. ST. FRANCIS HOTEL SAN FRANCISCO.

Again reports are sketchy, and possibly Lagron and Kelley were acting without the approval of Tannus. No one was very clear as to what could be gained by lodging a protest after the race was over, but apparently some of the National Airways group expected to use it as a foundation for an action for damages. Some of the race officials publicly commented on the display of bad taste in lodging a protest at a time while the search for the missing *Miss Doran* and *Golden Eagle* was in progress.

If the cruising range of the airplanes had been calculated as stated in the protesting telegram of Kelley and Lagron, the 90-mile-per-hour cruising speed would have dictated a 26.6 hour flight to cover the 2,400 miles. At a rate of 13 gallons per hour this would result in usage of 345 gallons. The 15 percent safety margin would require 52 more gallons for a total of 397 gallons. If the fuel capacity for all the planes had been calculated on that basis the 397-gallon requirement would certainly have been listed in the rules for the race. Furthermore there would have been no point in running flight tests on the planes if the conditions had been predetermined. On that basis the committee would have automatically disqualified the *El Encanto* with 360 gallons, the *Pabco Pacific Flyer* with 380 gallons, the *Golden Eagle* with 350 gallons, and the *City of Peoria* with 368 gallons.

It is interesting that the protestors named only the *Golden Eagle*, which was missing. The *El Encanto* and *Pabco Pacific Flyer*, though both damaged, were still available at the Oakland Airport for inspection.

After all the claims and counterclaims are sifted, in the absence of little verified evidence, I have attempted to reconstruct events with a minimum of assumptions.

First, the committee logically used a fixed rate of fuel consumption for the Wright J–5 of 13 gallons per hour. The Wright J–5 engine manual guaranteed fuel consumption as 0.53 pounds per horsepower at normal rpm. Normal cruise would be 75 percent of full power or approximately 168 horsepower. This results in consumption of about 89 pounds of fuel per hour. As aviation gasoline weighs from 6.5 to 7.0 pounds per gallon the guaranteed rate would be 12 ½ to 13 ¾ gallons per hour. The 13-gallon-per-hour rate was a good average.

The cruising speeds of the aircraft varied considerably. Obviously it would not make sense to use a fixed cruising speed for all entrants. Test flights were a crude method of establishing a cruising speed and range. The distance used for calculations was 2,400 miles. Normal cruising speed for the *Golden Eagle* was 118 miles per hour, but under the heavy load used in the race, the calculated speed was probably about 105 or slightly higher. This would require a total of 340 gallons including the safety requirement. With a 350 gallon capacity the *Golden Eagle* passed. The *City of Peoria* had a capacity of 368 gallons. As previously stated, using the 90-mile-per-hour speed, a total of 398 gallons would be required. Even by stretching the cruising speed to 95 miles per hour, the *City of Peoria* would be nine gallons short. All in all, it appears the race committee did Parkhurst and Lowes a favor by disqualifying their plane.

In fairness to the *City of Peoria* crew and owners, it does appear that the rules were relaxed in the case of the *Pabco Pacific Flyer* and the *Aloha*. In both cases a cruising speed of 94 miles per hour would be required to comply with the rules, but the speed was listed as 84 miles per hour. This becomes more obvious when you realize the *Aloha* lost two hours in its flight and landed with only 20 minutes fuel supply remaining. It rightly should have had approximately two hours supply remaining even after losing the two hours.

The *Golden Eagle* and *Miss Doran* were well within the race requirements. The *Woolaroc* and *Oklahoma* appeared well within the rules, and this was proven by the four hours of fuel remaining in the *Woolaroc*'s tanks after arrival at Honolulu. The *El Encanto* required a cruising speed of 100 miles per hour to meet the requirements. This was about right as it was the smallest and lightest plane in the race. The *Dallas Spirit* had far more range than needed to meet the requirements.

Though Charlie Parkhurst and Ralph Lowes were not allowed to try for the money or the glory of the Dole race, they partially achieved S. F. Tannus's original purpose in entering the race by obtaining more than their share of publicity. They continued their efforts to protest, but when the press no longer treated their antics as front page news they quietly dropped out of sight. Glenn Romkey and Lt. Robert Martin returned the Air King to Lomax, Illinois. Romkey claimed speeds of 103 to 110 miles per hour during the trip home, but no log was kept of the trip. Also the flight home was made with less than full loads and probably with west to east tailwinds.

After the excitement of the race had subsided somewhat the National Airways officials were still determined to obtain more publicity. On Monday, 22 August, an interview with Bernard Kelley and Ralph Lowes was held and reported on page one of the Peoria *Journal*. The article follows:

PEORIA PLANE VICTIM OF BAD DEAL–KELLEY
WAS FAVORED IN ILL FATED RACE TO HAWAII
Charges that the "City of Peoria" plane, entered in the Dole flight to Hawaii, was disqualified as a result of a frame-up by a gambling clique were made by Bernard Kelley, attorney for the National Airlines System, which built the plane. Kelley returned today from San Francisco together with Lt. Ralph C. Lowes, Jr., navigator of the Peoria plane, and Edward Lagron, advertising manager of the company. "It was a rotten deal for us throughout," Mr. Kelley said, as he elaborated on a formal statement which appears elsewhere in this article. "We are firmly convinced that gamblers wanted to take over our entry because the 'City of Peoria' was the favorite in the race to win."
SHORT NOTICE
"We were disqualified only 25 minutes before the plane was to takeoff," he added. "The excuse was that our gas supply was insufficient. This despite the fact that our plane carried 368 gallons and the "El Encanto" and "Golden Eagle" but 360 and 350 gallons respectively and our plane was faster than either of them. When I pointed out this fact to the officials one of them was shaking so badly he could scarcely talk. It was the most poorly managed affair we have ever had anything to contend with." Lt. Lowes was the most anxious to refute stories which, he said, had gained wide credence, to the affect that Parkhurst was yellow. Lt. Parkhurst was the pilot of the Peoria plane.
PRAISES PARKHURST
"I want to state emphatically that Lt. Parkhurst is anything but yellow," Lowes told the Journal. "If ever a man showed courage in the face of obstacles, he was the one. I think I am qualified to talk on this point having flown with him throughout preparations for the flight." According to Lt. Lowes and Mr. Kelley, Lt. Parkhurst is to leave San Francisco for the east late today or tomorrow. They said he would likely bring the plane to Peoria. He will take the southern route and make the hop by easy jumps, they said.
DESCRIBES NAME CHANGE
Mr. Kelley also said he wished to correct the impression gained from the news stories that the name "City of Peoria" was removed from the plane entirely and Air King substituted throughout. It was necessary to put on a new cowl on the plane and it was impossible to use a large enough lettering on it he explained but the name, the "City of Peoria" appeared in large letters on the plane elsewhere. "The Peoria plane received an unusually large amount of publicity," said Lt. Lowes. "There were scores of former Peoria people at the space and they all greeted us warmly." Mr. Kelley's statements to the Journal follows: "There have been so many rumors and counter rumors as regards the 'City of Peoria' that we deemed it necessary to issue the following statement: The Air King biplane, christened 'City of Peoria,' left Lomax, Illinois Monday evening August 8th. A nonstop flight was not attempted for the reason that the trip was to be used as a series of tests so that necessary alterations, if they were needed, would be made to the motor and plane, etc. The plane arrived at the Oakland airport Thursday, August 10th, in the afternoon. Entries there were possibly not too prepared to go at the time so

through an agreement, which all pilots signed, the flight was postponed until the following Tuesday. This postponement came as a great relief to each and every entry as it gave time and opportunity for more careful preparations. Each contestant was subjected to two tests; the first being the navigation test, and the second, half load test. The first test was conducted by Lt. Benjamin Wyatt of the USN, which our navigator, Ralph Lowes, passed 100%, being off course less than 100 yards in a distance of 25 miles. A fact which brought forth high praise from the examining officer. The second test, that of half load test, was equally gratifying, the ship taking off in 14 seconds carrying 134 gallons of gasoline, pilot, navigator and full equipment. This being 7 seconds less than any other ship on the field. From this time on until the date set for hop off every minute was given over to preparation.

RUMORS SHOWN FALSE

"Less than 24 hours from what was to be the beginning of the race, rumors reached us that there had been some discussion as to whether or not we were carrying a sufficient supply of gasoline. This rumor had it that the 'City of Peoria' had a cruising speed of 80 MPH. This being true, 368 gallons of gasoline, which was our capacity, would be insufficient. However, we knew that the cruising speed of the 'City of Peoria' was over 80 MPH. Just to satisfy ourselves and without being officially requested to do so, we ran a special test over a measured course, the time being checked by Edward Lagron, Captain Mosher, Ralph Lowes, Lt. George Noville, who was with Byrd on his New York to Paris flight, and myself. This test proved conclusively that the cruising speed was 90 MPH at 1600 RPM or about 120 to 135 top speed. Even figuring our cruising speed at 95 MPH, 368 gallons of gas gave us a safety margin of 18% or 3% more than was required under the regulation governing the race. [Actually at 95 mph a total of 25 ¼ would be required, and 328 gallons of fuel would be consumed. A total capacity of 368 gallons leaves 40 gallons or 12 percent reserve, not 18 percent as Kelley stated]. Not having heard anything from the committee whatsoever and feeling satisfied by the tests we conducted, we put it all down to rumor and forgot about the matter.

OTHERS FAVORED

"At 11:30 all ships took their place on the starting line, the 'City of Peoria' among them. At 11:35 when Mr. Lagron went to headquarters to get our certificate we were told that the 'City of Peoria' was disqualified because in their opinion it was carrying insufficient gas. We immediately pointed out that the 'El Encanto' was carrying only 360 gallons of gas or 8 gallons less than the 'City of Peoria' and that the 'Golden Eagle' was carrying 350 gallons of gas or 18 gallons less than the 'City of Peoria,' but to no avail. We threatened to send the ship anyway and were informed that ones pilot license would be revoked, that we would not be considered qualified to receive any prize money, and that we would be subject to a fine for having violated rules of the Department of Commerce. If we had been advised 6 hours prior to takeoff, we could have met any regulation of qualification of the committee. Tanks of any size would have been added in that time. The real reason for our disqualification we do not know. We were told by people on the field that it was probably due to the ring of gambling, field politics, and competitive jealousies. We do know that the 'City of Peoria' was considered to be a very capable and fast ship by such men as Art Starbuck, Bob Fowler, George Noble, Ernie Smith, and a host of other celebrities in the aviation world.

We feel satisfied that the 'City of Peoria' could have won. We are proud of the boys and proud of the ship. The name 'City of Peoria' was on the first page of every metropolitan newspaper for weeks but when we count the cost and realize that out of 15 entries only 2 ships are left, the 'City of Peoria' and 'Oklahoma,' other than those 2 reaching the goal, that out of 21 pilots and navigators, 10 are probably dead. [Actually of the fifteen entrants in addition to the four he mentioned the *El Encanto* was damaged and later repaired, the *Detroit Messenger* was at Oakland and in flying condition, the *Miss Hollydale* was flying at Long Beach, and Bob Fowler, one of the fifteen, never had a plane to begin with.] We feel that after all we were fortunate. We feel grateful to those people who contributed in the neighborhood of $4,000. We feel grateful to Mr. Tannus of the National Airways System who spent $20,000 in the building and equipping of the 'City of Peoria' and who on being questioned commented the cost is nothing in that two Peoria boys escaped the ill fortune of other entries."

Bernard Kelley
Attorney National Airways System

Bernard Kelley must have underestimated his readers as his statement was riddled with falsehoods and errors. Thus ended the saga of the *City of Peoria* in the Dole race. The National Airways System and the airplane continued to make news, but that is another story.

13

SEARCH AND FAILURE

By the time Marty Jensen touched down at Honolulu in the late afternoon of Wednesday, 17 August, the rumor was strong that the other two entrants were down in the Pacific. Both Goebel and Jensen reported they never saw another contestant after passing the Farallone Islands. Those in the know were especially worried about the *Golden Eagle* because it should have arrived ahead of all the others. It was a well-built plane, had been extensively tested for weeks prior to the race, and had an experienced crew. The *Miss Doran*, on the other hand, was considered rather slow but very reliable and well proven; though burdened with the extra weight of a passenger, it still had an excellent chance of safely reaching the islands. As the afternoon faded into evening the lights were turned on at Wheeler Field on the chance that one or both of the missing planes would still arrive. But as darkness settled it was evident to most that the *Golden Eagle* and *Miss Doran* were down. The *Golden Eagle* could be expected to remain aloft about 29 to 30 hours if the engine was throttled back to conserve fuel. The *Miss Doran*, with a larger fuel supply, could possibly fly for 33 to 34 hours, with careful use of the throttle, but by nightfall it was certain that both planes were down. The newspapers were reporting the *Golden Eagle* had been seen turning north instead of west after it cleared the Golden Gate. This report was rapidly disproved as Lee Schoenhair had accompanied the *Golden Eagle* for more than 100 miles out over the Pacific before turning back to Oakland. At that point, 60 miles past the Farallones, Schoenhair reported, all was well.

Early on Thursday morning the Army and Navy dispatched all available planes to search the area surrounding Honolulu. The morning edition of the Honolulu *Star Bulletin* headline read "Forty-two Naval Vessels Search Sea, Hope Is Still Alive." A smaller headline stated "Dole Offers Reward of $10,000 Per Each Plane Crew."

Japanese fishing vessels were alerted, and all commercial ships in the area were asked to keep a lookout. A total of 120 sampams were involved in the search of the island area. The Navy armada included seven destroyers from San Diego, four destroyers enroute from Honolulu to Seattle, twenty-three submarines and three submarine tenders from Pearl Harbor, and the aircraft carrier U. S. S. *Langley* and the aircraft tender U.S.S. *Aroostook* out of San Diego.

Both Goebel and Jensen returned to Wheeler Field early in the morning of 18 August. After repairing the damage inflicted by crowds and souvenir hunters on the *Woolaroc* and *Aloha* they both flew out to sea to help with the search. Marty Jensen's wife, Peg, accompanied him, and they flew for five hours from Kauai to the big island of Hawaii and 200 miles out to sea without seeing any trace of the lost planes. When interviewed Jensen stated "I will not rest. I have no plans, there is only one thought in my mind and that is to save my buddies." Search flights were made also at the San Francisco end, as many people felt the missing fliers could easily have gone down shortly after takeoff.

Late Thursday afternoon a false report was received that the *Miss Doran* had been located and all aboard had been rescued. The message, from a part-time correspondent and Maui deputy tax assessor, J. Olwiera Jr., read "Pedlar plane found at Honomanu Bay near Keanae. All on board taken off."

The Honolulu *Advertiser* published the report immediately in an extra without checking for authenticity. At the same time they wired Olwiera for additional details and contacted their regular correspondent, John Morrow, at Wailuku, but no reports were received for two hours. About 8:00 P.M. Morrow replied that the reported plane was probably a gaudily painted launch owned by Dave Flenning, who was fishing in the vicinity and who had just landed at Hana. Meanwhile Olwiera sent a second message reading "Hold report re landing Pedlar plane. Latest report Pedlar drifting toward Hana Sampam Makoiwa sent to rescue. Foss of Olinda reports sighting a plane on horizon on Muelo at 6 P.M."

Morrow sent another message stating "Cory Pogue maintains plane red white and blue seen by him but drifting toward Nahiku. Says most certain except drifting too fast for unmotored craft. Sampam now within ten miles of supposed craft." At 8:30 P.M. Olwiera sent an explanation. "First informer Miss Wilhelm of Kallua. She reported receiving telephone message from Honomanu that plane landed Honomanu occupants being taken off. Coville Pogue, Kailua, reports that he was sure it was a plane and followed it from Kailua to Keanae. Plane flying white kite about 150 feet high. Foss of Olinda saw a plane off Muelo at 6 P.M. on horizon." Later reports confirmed that what had been identified as a red, white, and blue plane was indeed a fishing launch. No explanation was made concerning the report that the people had been rescued or of the white kite supposedly flown from the downed plane.

Another report stated Pedlar had been picked up off of Kakuku, but this was soon proved to be false.

The Thursday evening edition of the Honolulu *Star Bulletin* also had a small article stating that the luau, to be given by James Dole on Friday 19 August, was indefinitely postponed.

Meanwhile back on the mainland Capt. Frederick A. Giles, in his Hess Bluebird, took off from Detroit on the first leg of his flight. Even though the race was over Captain Giles still planned to complete an 11,000-mile flight from Detroit to Australia. He left the Ford Airport near Detroit in a rainstorm, planning to stop at Chicago, Omaha, Cheyenne, and Salt Lake City before flying to Oakland. From there he still planned to try for Hawaii.

On Thursday afternoon, 18 August, Bill Malloska was interviewed in his room in the Young Hotel in Honolulu. He was completely heartbroken over the apparent loss of the *Miss Doran* and his close friends in the crew. He too offered a 10,000-dollar reward for any information leading to the rescue of his friends. He felt that the only explanation was that the *Miss Doran* had caught on fire. Otherwise, he reasoned, the fuel could have been dumped and the empty tanks would have kept the plane afloat for weeks. He displayed the last radiograms he received from Mildred Doran. The first read "Everything all fixed up fine see you Wednesday," the second, "Have a new navigator Lawing didn't pass. Everything O.K. See you Wednesday. Mildred Doran."

James Dole was also interviewed and provided a statement for the press. "Two things are already shown by this flight. First that the chance taken by Lindbergh in flying without a radio sending device and taken by three of the four fliers in the Dole Race to Honolulu without radio sending devices is too hazardous. Second that what is required and what must be invented by someone is a suitable sending device which is capable of being used by a plane if forced down in the water."

William Randolph Hearst added to the growing list of rewards being offered for information on the lost fliers, a total that reached 60,000 dollars by Friday, 19 August. Also on Friday, a report was received that an amateur wireless operator living in Alhambra, California, intercepted a message reporting the finding at sea of a derelict airplane and its life raft with one man and the body of a woman. The message was quoted as "A passenger ship reports that a girl was found dead and a man alive in a life raft at 9:12 A.M. today. The ship took the raft up and sank the plane at site." This message was rapidly proven false, and hope was dashed again.

In the Oakland–San Francisco area the various ground crew members and backers of the *Miss Doran* and *Golden Eagle* tried to analyze the reports that had been received. Much as they didn't want to admit it, there was a strong possibility the missing planes had gone down within a few hundred miles of the takeoff point. The Navy had already started a massive search operation off the coast of California. In San Diego, Captain John Tower, skipper of the aircraft carrier U.S.S. *Langley*, had prepared well in advance of the flight, on the assumption that at least one plane would be lost. Having been skipper of the NC-3, one of the Navy aircraft that failed to complete the Atlantic crossing in 1919, he was well aware of the hazards of overwater flying and the relatively small chance of spotting a downed aircraft in an immense ocean. He ordered the *Langley* to head for the Farallones at top speed, there to rendezvous with the Navy tender *Aroostook*. At the same time a flotilla was dispatched from San Francisco consisting of the cruiser U.S.S. *Omaha* and the destroyers U.S.S. *Farenholt*, *Kidder*, and *Hull*. Three submarines joined them along with the Coast Guard vessels *Takokia* and *Shawnee*.

William Randolph Hearst made an offer to help that was eagerly accepted by Captain Tower. Through the San Francisco *Examiner*, a seagoing tug was chartered that steamed out to contact the *Langley*. Both Ken Jay of Lockheed and Denham Scott, brother of Gordon Scott, were on board. They met the *Langley* and were taken on board to serve as advisors to Captain Tower during the search.

For ten days the U. S. Navy ships and airplanes combed the Pacific. In all they covered 540,000 square miles, but not one shred of wreckage was located. During this time, Bill Erwin and Alvin Eichwoldt were also lost on their belated attempt to reach Hawaii. Their crash location was known within a comparatively few miles based on their radio signals and sightings by ships. The Navy searched this area minutely but again drew a complete blank. After ten days the official search was called off, but all ships continued to maintain a lookout. To this day no identifiable part of any of the three lost planes has ever been located.

14

DALLAS SPIRIT TO THE RESCUE

Shortly after its successful takeoff in the Pacific Air Race on 16 August, the *Dallas Spirit* was spotted returning to the Oakland Airport. The crowd was not too surprised, as they had already watched the return of the *Oklahoma* and the *Miss Doran*. As the *Dallas Spirit* flew over the field preparing to land, the crowd could see that a large piece of fabric was stripped from the right side of the plane. Long shreds and strips of fabric were streaming back, threatening to become entangled in the horizontal stabilizer and elevator. The pilots, mechanics, and officials were extremely worried, not so much by the fabric streamers, but by the fact the airplane was overloaded and no provisions for dumping the excess fuel had been made. A blown tire, weak landing gear, or any number of minor mishaps during landing could result in a fiery crash. Added to the danger, of course, were the thousands of spectators milling about on the field and near the runway. The safest procedure under the circumstances would have been for Bill Erwin to fly around for many hours burning off fuel and at the same time to throw overboard all loose items that could be spared from the cabin area. This would have lowered the aircraft weight to a near-safe level and permitted a normal landing. But Bill Erwin had no way of telling how badly the rear fuselage was damaged, and he assumed there was a reasonable chance of effecting a speedy repair, allowing him to remain in the race. He, therefore, elected to attempt landing one of the most overloaded single-engine aircraft ever flown. Captain Erwin did a superb job and touched down gently on the first try. As soon as the plane rolled to a stop, Erwin was met by E. M. Dealey, a reporter covering Erwin's flight and his close personal friend. "Got anything to eat?" said Erwin. Dealey took him over to his old Hudson car parked next to the runway and gave him a few bananas.

After a short investigation the cause for the failure was determined. Alvin Eichwoldt, the navigator, had cut a trap door in the bottom of the fuselage to enable him to drop smoke bombs during the flight. This was a standard method of determining wind drift from an airplane. The door was closed during takeoff, but apparently either the force of the wind or the vibration of the long takeoff roll caused it to open, allowing air to rush through the rear of the fuselage. Very quickly the pressure built up, a weak spot in the fuselage fabric failed, and the fabric started to rip off in long strips. It probably sounded worse than it was, and Erwin, assuming the problem could only get worse, decided to go back to terra firma as soon as possible. After landing, the airplane was inspected and it was decided that, even if it were possible to repair the fabric in a comparatively short time, Erwin would be at least three hours behind the leaders. As most of the aircraft were capable of approximately the same speeds the chances of overcoming a three-hour lead were nil. Erwin and Eichwoldt reluctantly announced they were out of the race.

By late afternoon of the following day everyone was forced to admit the *Golden Eagle* and the *Miss Doran* were down somewhere in the vast Pacific. Reports from ships and first reports from Goebel and Jensen on their arrival at Honolulu indicated the weather had not been too bad. Large areas of the ocean had been covered with heavy cloud layers, and some localized rain showers had been encountered. There was certainly a good chance that one or both of the downed crews had been successful in crash-landings on the ocean and were afloat somewhere in their rafts.

Bill Erwin and Alvin Eichwoldt were still keyed up from the recent events, and both felt they would like to attempt a Pacific flight even though the prizes had already been won. The more they talked the more they felt it was worth a try, not only for the sheer thrill of it, but also to search for their friends who were lost. To add additional pressure on Erwin, the day after the race he received a strongly worded telegram from his backers in Dallas, criticizing him for not continuing the flight and urging him to try again. Billy Parker tried his best to talk Erwin out of it, but the answer was that the backers had paid for the flight and he felt he should give them their money's worth and make another attempt. He also still had hopes of continuing on to Hong Kong to complete the originally planned flight from Dallas to the Orient. Marty Jensen had tried to convince him that no airport in the Hawaiian Islands had runways long enough to handle the takeoff of a heavily loaded airplane but Erwin still wanted to try it. If he would be successful, he felt he would recoup much of the money he and his Texas backers had already invested. Accordingly he announced his plans to take off on 19 August and to follow, as close as possible, what he assumed to be the routes of the *Golden Eagle* and the *Miss Doran*.

E. M. Dealey, reporter for a Dallas newspaper who was assigned to cover Captain Erwin's efforts in the Pacific Air Race, was also acting as an unofficial business manager for the *Dallas Spirit* team. He tried repeatedly to dissuade Erwin from taking off. Many others tried as well but were also unsuccessful. On 19 August, Dealey drove Erwin and Eichwoldt to the Oakland Airport. Halfway to the field they were met by two officials of the National Aeronautics Committee for the Pacific Air Race, Harry E. MacConaughey, vice-president and San Francisco manager of the Hawaiian Pineapple Company, and Capt. C. W. Sounders, operating head of the Matson Navigation Company. Both spent considerable time trying to convince Erwin to change his mind but could not.

Against all advice, Bill Erwin and Alvin Eichwoldt took off a second time at 2:15 P.M., 19 August 1927. This time their plane weighed 5,600 pounds as it was loaded with even more fuel, 480 gallons, than at the start of the Pacific Air Race. It was reported to be the heaviest load any single-engine plane had ever lifted up to that time. Erwin had heeded some of his friends' advice and installed a shortwave radio, operating at 33.1 meters. By use of the radio he planned to keep a running log throughout the flight. This was probably the first time an actual log was maintained on any overocean flight. The two adventurers were in great spirits when they took off and started sending messages almost immediately. The complete log follows:

2:20–2:50 P.M. GOING STRONG WE ARE PASSING THE DOCKS WE'LL SEE THE LIGHT SHIP SOON. WE ARE CARRYING THE TAIL HIGH AT 1700 AND WE ARE MAKING CLOSE TO 100 MPH AIRSPEED. WILL CALL AGAIN WHEN PASSING LIGHT SHIP.

WE ARE PASSING POINT LOBOS [Golden Gate] NOW.

WE ARE NOW PASSING THE LIGHT SHIP AND SEE THE TWO FLAG SIGNALS WHICH MEAN THAT YOU BUMS ARE GETTING US AND WE CAN SEE THE FARALLONES AHEAD. FROM NOW ON I WILL DOUBLE UP [indicating increased power] SO YOU CAN COPY BETTER AND I KNOW MY SENDING IS NONE TOO GOOD. TELL MCALLISTER THAT THE SET IS WORKING FINE. LOVE TO MA. WE ARE FLYING AT 300 FT. AND UNDER THE FOG WITH 30 MILES VISIBILITY NOW.

2:55 P.M. OVERCAST STRATA OVER US. CLOUDY BUT IT LOOKS LIKE CLEARING FARTHER AHEAD. THAT LAST MEANS THE BARON IS SENDING. TELL EDDIE BLOW THAT HIS JOB ON THE WINDOW IS FINE. WE ARE TURNING UP 1650 RPM AND MAKING 95 AIRSPEED. ALL INSTRUMENTS WORKING FINE WILL SAY MORE LATER. REGARDS TO LT. WYATT.

3:10 P.M. OUR CEILING IS INCREASING AND THE SUN IS BREAKING THROUGH.

3:28 P.M. BILL AND I BOTH SEND OUR BEST WISHES TO MR. AND MRS. DEALEY AND TO ALL THE LARGE CROWD OF WELL WISHERS THAT SAW US OFF.

3:33 P.M. IKE HAD A DRINK OF WATER.

3:49 P.M. THE CEILING IS NOW 700 FT. WE ARE FLYING AT 500 FT. WE HAVEN'T SEEN ANYTHING SINCE THE FARALLONES AND ALL IS OK EXCEPT BILL JUST SNEEZED. WE ARE KEEPING A SHARP LOOKOUT FOR THE DORAN PLANE ALSO THE GOLDEN EAGLE. WILL CALL YOU AGAIN LATER.

4:20 P.M. WE JUST PASSED CLOSE TO A RAIN SQUALL. THE AIR IS A LITTLE BUMPY IN THIS VICINITY. WE SOON LEFT IT BEHIND HOWEVER VERY CLEAR AHEAD.

4:35 P.M. WE ADJUSTED OUR ANTENNA FOR MORE RADIATION. THE VISIBILITY IS VERY GOOD. WE ARE ABLE TO COVER 80 MILES.

4:50 P.M. TELL DEALEY THAT BILL WANTS TO KNOW WHERE THE NOODLE FACTORY IS.

5:05 P.M. WE SEE A SHIP AHEAD OF US PRESUMABLY THE MANA. WE WILL GO DOWN CLOSE AND WAVE TO THEM.

5:11 P.M. PLANE JUST PASSED THE STEAMSHIP MANA AT 5:10 COAST TIME AND DIPPED IN SALUTE. THEY ANSWERED ON THE WHISTLE. OF COURSE WE COULD NOT HEAR IT BUT WE SAW THE STEAM. WE MIGHT PICK UP THE SQUADRON OF DESTROYERS BEFORE DARK BUT THAT DEPENDS ON THEIR SPEED. ALL OKAY. [Position of the *Mana* was 240 miles from San Francisco, which indicates the *Dallas Spirit* was averaging 82 miles per hour.]

5:28 P.M. JUST PASSED THE DESTROYER GOING TOWARD SAN FRANCISCO. THE DESTROYER WAS NOT US. WE ARE BOUND FOR HONOLULU. THE DESTROYER WAS TOO FAR AWAY FOR US TO MAKE HIS NUMBER. NOTHING ELSE IN SIGHT.

5:36 P.M. AT 5:30 P.M. WE ARE PASSING A VESSEL THAT HAS AN APPEARANCE OF AN OIL TANKER ON THE NORTH OF US AND TWO MINUTES LATER WE SAW ANOTHER CRAFT SOUTH OF US. WE CAN SEE SMOKE FROM STILL ANOTHER STEAMER SOUTH OF US.

5:45 P.M. JUST SAW A RUM RUNNER ON THE LEFT AND HAD A HELL OF A TIME KEEPING IKE IN—BILL.

5:57 P.M. WE ARE NOW ABOUT TO HAVE SUPPER. WILL CALL YOU AGAIN AFTER SUPPER.

6:05 P.M. PLEASE TELL THE GENTLEMAN WHO FURNISHED OUR LUNCH THAT IT IS FINE BUT WE CAN'T FIND THE TOOTHPICKS— BILL.

6:54 P.M. JUST HAD A SANDWICH APIECE AND A CUP OF COFFEE AND IT SURE WENT GOOD. WE CHANGED COURSE AT 6:40 P.M. TO $244\frac{1}{2}$ TRUE. POSITION AT THAT TIME LATITUDE 35 DEGREES 30 MINUTES NORTH 130 WEST.

7:10 P.M. THE WEATHER IS PART CLOUDY WITH A SMOOTH SEA. VISIBILITY ABOUT 30 MILES. HAVE SEEN NO WRECKAGE OR ANYTHING THAT MIGHT BE EITHER OF THE ONES WE ARE LOOKING FOR. THE VISIBILITY IS STILL VERY GOOD. EVERYTHING WITH US OKAY. WE ARE FLYING AT 900 FT.

8:00 P.M. IT IS NOW GETTING DARK AND WE APPARENTLY WILL NOT BE ABLE TO SEE MUCH UNTIL MORNING.

The messages ended for approximately an hour. During that period there were times when Eichwoldt apparently held the wireless key down without sending a coded message. The experienced radio operators on the shore felt that the *Dallas Spirit* had entered a storm area and that the crew probably had their hands full. There was considerable variation in the pitch of the radio signal being transmitted. As the power was supplied by a wind-driven generator with no form of speed regulation, the frequency or sound level of the output would vary with the speed of the airplane. As the speed increased the pitch of the sound would also rise. As the plane climbed or dove the pitch or frequency of the signal would decrease or increase. During a cruising condition the signal would normally be a steady hum.

The pitch varied for some time while the listeners on ship and shore imagined the worst. Suddenly about 8:50 P.M. it increased noticeably. Shortly after that pieces of messages came through but were rather garbled. For a short period, parts such as "Came out of it" and "We are in a tail spin" were picked up. Then a relatively clear message was reported by most of the listening stations. As near as can be determined it read:

SOS—WE ARE IN A TAIL SPIN—WE CAME OUT OF IT OKAY BUT WE'RE SURE SCARED. IT WAS A CLOSE CALL. I THOUGHT IT WAS ALL OVER BUT CAME OUT OF IT. THE LIGHT ON THE INSTRUMENT BOARD WENT OUT AND IT WAS SO DARK THAT BILL COU. . . .

The last word was never finished. A short while later another report was picked up which read: "WE'RE IN ANOTHER TAIL SPIN." Then silence.

The final grim total of fatalities attributed to the Pacific Air Race was complete. Three died in crashes preceding the race, five were lost during the actual race, and two more were lost in the aftermath for a total sacrifice of ten.

15

THE SEARCH CONTINUES

The loss of the prototype Lockheed Vega *Golden Eagle* was almost a fatal blow to the young Lockheed Aircraft Company. The company backers had gambled their entire future on winning the Dole race and garnering national publicity for their revolutionary design. A win would demonstrate to the world the superiority of their model Vega and would undoubtedly result in many orders for planes. Not only were they counting on a first place in the race, but, due to the proven performance of the Vega, they were confident of beating the nearest competitor by many hours. So sure were they of winning that they had even sold the plane to William Randolph Hearst at a loss. When the *Golden Eagle* was lost in the Pacific the Lockheed Company did not have any firm orders for the Vega model on their books, and trying to sell a new airplane, identical to one that had received world-wide publicity for disappearing over the Pacific, was an almost impossible task. But the group of Lockheed employees still had faith in their product and were convinced the *Golden Eagle*'s loss could not be traced to any fault of the airplane. They had already started building Vega number two, and they now worked even harder to complete and test fly it so it could be used as a demonstrator. Fortunately within a short time Hubert Wilkins, noted explorer, placed an order for the second Vega to be used for an upcoming Arctic Flight. Rumor had it that Wilkins had seen the *Golden Eagle* take off in the Dole race and had been convinced that it was the most promising design of 1927. This order kept the infant company going through the spring of 1928.

Denham Scott, brother of the *Golden Eagle*'s navigator, was hired by Lockheed and became the twenty-sixth person on their payroll. After working for a few months he was surprised by a visitor, Marty Jensen. Denham Scott, Jensen, and Ken Jay of Lockheed spent many long hours discussing the loss of the *Golden Eagle*. They convinced themselves that the plane could have reached Hawaii and either crashed on the big island or overshot its mark falling into the sea somewhere west of the islands. Jensen had been contacted by an islander who ridiculed his story of being lost until noon on Wednesday 17 August. He insisted Jensen had some ulterior motive for his story. The islander was most insistent that he himself had seen Jensen's yellow plane cross the coastline of the island of Hawaii on a path from the mainland to Honolulu at 11:00 A.M. on the morning of the seventeenth. After much questioning by Jensen the man said he even remembered the registration number of Jensen's plane—NX–913—on the wing. As the *Aloha's* number was NX–914, and the plane was yellow, the man could be telling the truth, as he thought he saw it, but Jensen knew positively that he and Paul Schluter were more than 200 miles from Hawaii at 11:00 A.M. that Wednesday. However, the *Golden Eagle* was an orange monoplane numbered NX–913. The only other plane unaccounted for, the *Miss Doran*, was a biplane, was painted a rather gaudy red, white, and blue and was number NX–2915. The more Jensen thought about it the more logical it seemed that the *Golden Eagle* and the *Aloha* could be mistaken for each other, but the *Miss Doran* should be readily identifiable. Another strong point of evidence was the fact the islander did not mention the large lettering, ALOHA, on the fuselage of Jensen's plane. If the plane had been low enough to read the registration numbers he surely would have noticed the extremely large name painted on both sides of the fuselage. The *Golden Eagle* also had its name on the fuselage but in very small letters that could never be read from the ground. All in all, evidence seemed rather strong that the man had truly seen the *Golden Eagle*. After hearing substantially the same story, though not in quite as much detail, from a few others Jensen decided there must be some truth in it and, on his next visit to the mainland, contacted Denham Scott. Both Jay and Scott felt it was worth investigating, so early in 1928 Scott left his job at Lockheed and signed on as a crew member on the *City of Los Angeles*, a steamer bound for Hawaii. Denham Scott was still rated as an able-bodied seaman and in those lean times he saw no reason for paying the cost of a trip across the Pacific if he could ride free.

After arrival in Hawaii he spent a total of five months following leads and rumors concerning a plane crash on the big island of Hawaii. Marty Jensen had returned to his old job of flying for the Lewis Hawaiian Tours Company. The only difference was he now flew the reconditioned *Aloha* instead of the old Ryan of prerace days. The Breese had been converted from its Dole race configuration to the standard, passenger-carrying, cabin monoplane. At every opportunity Jensen allowed Denham Scott to ride along and look for the lost *Golden Eagle*. In return, Scott acted as barker for Jensen to sell rides on weekends in Honolulu.

During his off-hours Scott tried to chase down every rumor that he heard concerning a lost airplane. Quite a few people claimed to have heard a plane on 17 August flying from the sea toward the mountains. Others claimed to have seen flares that night and on a few succeeding nights on the slopes of Mauna Loa, the huge active volcano on the island of Hawaii that reached a height of 13,680 feet. A sister peak, Mauna Kea, rising to 13,796 feet, was located about 25 miles north. Both of these mountains were usually shrouded in clouds.

A glance at the map shows Mauna Loa is about 175 miles southeast of Honolulu or about two degrees longitude and two degrees latitude off of a direct great circle course from San Francisco to Honolulu. An error of less than five degrees in the compass course, a slight error in the originally calculated compass deviation, or an error of five miles per hour in wind drift could have caused the *Golden Eagle* to be off course this small amount. The *Golden Eagle* was equipped with a radio receiver, which should have allowed Jack Frost and Gordon Scott to follow the radio signals from Wheeler Field, as Goebel had done in his *Woolaroc*. But the reliability of radios and compasses was none too good in 1927. No one knows if their radio functioned or if, like the Army fliers before them, they were forced to rely on dead reckoning for the entire flight. Another big question mark was the possible damage to instruments that may have been sustained in the *Golden Eagle*'s mishap in San Diego a few days before the race. In the rush to repair the damage possibly some errors in the instruments could have gone undetected. All of these possibilities were considered by Denham Scott as he spent many weeks criss-crossing Hawaii to interview witnesses. He finally narrowed his interest to a total of seventeen reasonably reliable witnesses. As he tells the story, "no two of them were of the same nationality," a fact that hindered the questioning considerably. Each of them, when questioned in detail, insisted they had seen flares on Mauna Loa on Wednesday, 17 August, and again on Sunday, 21 August. On the nights between, the mountains were entirely obscured by clouds. The location of each witness at the time of the sightings was established and by use of a surveyor's level and transit, bearings were laid out on a large map. All seventeen intersected in one small area at approximately the 11,000-foot level on Mauna Loa. This was a remote, uninhabited area consisting of volcanic rock and ash that would be extremely difficult to search. This further helped to convince Denham Scott that the *Golden Eagle* was the source of the flares. An altitude of 11,000 feet could easily be the height that Jack Frost would have been flying. However this reasoning ignored one strong piece of evidence. When the plane reported by the original witness crossed the coastline of Hawaii, he could read the registration number NX–913 on the wing. Possibly Frost's radio had failed or he would have been on a more direct course to Honolulu and would not be crossing the big island of Hawaii. He would probably have dropped down to a low altitude to identify the island he was approaching. After deciding that it was Hawaii and knowing that Mauna Loa and Mauna Kea were both between him and Wheeler Field, he would naturally climb. With the mountains shrouded in clouds and not being familiar with the area it is conceivable the *Golden Eagle* was flown into the side of Mauna Loa at about the 11,000-foot point. In any event, Denham Scott decided to act on that assumption. His investigations had already aroused the interest of many Army personnel stationed in the area. Capt. Elmer Block, commandant of one of the detachments stationed near Mauna Loa, was the most interested. Captain Block and one of his men, Sergeant Brown, had already tried to investigate the flares reported on Mauna Loa without success. When he heard that Scott was in the area he offered to help to equip another search party to investigate the slopes of Mauna Loa. With the help of seven volunteer soldiers, four volunteered Army mules, and numerous items of volunteered Army supplies Scott searched the slopes for about three months. No actual trace of the *Golden Eagle* was ever found, even though many erroneous reports were circulated that articles of clothing and burned-out flares had been discovered. To this day these erroneous reports are still mentioned in stories concerning the Pacific Air Race. After three months Denham Scott reached the conclusion that, if his brother and Jack Frost had really reached the island of Hawaii and crashed on Mauna Loa, they had probably been injured and after running out of flares had set fire to their plywood plane in an attempt to attract attention. This and the periodic flow of lava from the active volcano could account for the failure to locate any evidence of the crash.

Finally with time and money exhausted, Denham Scott gave up his quest to locate the *Golden Eagle* and returned to the mainland. But the mystery of the *Golden Eagle*'s disappearance has always remained in his mind. As they years went by he, his sister, Shelia, Ken Jay, Eddie Cooper, and many others of the original Lockheed crew spent countless hours and untold evenings trying to fathom the mystery. Originally Denham Scott felt his brother and Jack Frost reached Hawaii. But after his exhaustive search on Mauna Loa he reached a new conclusion. He felt the *Golden Eagle* had arrived over the Hawaiian chain earlier than expected and, at a high altitude, passed over the islands, which were hidden in the early morning fog and haze. Continuing westward they finally realized, too late, they had overshot their mark and run out of time and fuel needed to retrace their path. Under this theory the last flight of the *Golden Eagle* would be easy to imagine.

The problem could have started with the unfortunate accident at San Diego in which the landing gear and fuselage of the *Golden Eagle* were damaged. Repairs may have caused a slight deviation in the compass. Deviation is that slight difference between the true magnetic reading and the compass reading usually induced by metallic objects in the airplane such as generators, engines, and radios. A further slight deviation would have been introduced when the original radio was replaced with a small receiving set just an hour or two before the start of the race. Probably the substitute radio failed shortly after takeoff. During the long night they droned steadily westward with only an occasional star fix to check their position. They looked forward to dawn to allow Scott to obtain a more positive position check and a check on wind drift against the ocean surface. If their progress was better than anticipated they could have unwittingly passed over or close to Honolulu, which was still obscured by the early morning fog and haze. Assuming they were close to the islands, Frost started a cautious descent. When they finally broke out above the calm sea no land was in sight. Naturally they continued on their westerly heading. About midmorning, after the haze had dissipated enough to give them good visibility, Scott took a series of sun shots and drift readings on the waves below. They were actually a few hundred miles west of the islands and getting further away every minute. Jack Frost turned the *Golden Eagle* back toward the east, but by now their fate was sealed. When it came time to ditch the Vega in the sea, they probably hit the crest of a wave and overturned. Almost assuredly the fuselage broke open. The myriad safety devices—carbon dioxide operated flotation gear, dropable landing gear, life rafts, and all the rest—required a human hand to operate. Frost and Scott were probably stunned by the crash, and, with the fuselage broken open, the *Golden Eagle* would have sunk rapidly without a trace.

Now it is sixty years since the *Golden Eagle* made its last flight. Both Denham Scott and Eddie Cooper have had much time to think, and they jointly reached a third, and what they considered a true, version of the fate of the *Golden Eagle*.

Jack Frost was an experienced wartime pilot and an extremely personable and likable young man. However from 1922 to 1927 he had given up flying to concentrate on his business enterprises. When Ken Jay called him to ask if he would be interested in being a crew member on the Lockheed Vega in the Dole race, he jumped at the chance and, as we know, was accepted by Hearst and Rochlen. Acceptance was based more on Ken Jay's strong endorsement and Jack Frost's personality than on his flying ability. Frost tried to regain his skill as a pilot, but in the few short weeks before the race he fought a losing battle. Also the Vega was a high-performance airplane unlike the "low and slow" World War 1 planes Frost was accustomed to. A third and possibly fatal factor would be introduced— night flying. Frost had no night flying experience at all and had little opportunity to acquire any before the race. Denham Scott and Eddie Cooper both agreed these points are the keys to the loss of the *Golden Eagle*. Flying at night, without a horizon to guide you through patches of cloud or haze, can be extremely difficult for an experienced pilot. Marty Jensen spun three times during his crossing and admits it was only his long experience at stunt flying that saved him. Art Goebel, though he was able to stay above the clouds most of the time all the way to Hawaii, attributed his success to his stunt flying experience. All Jack Frost had to do was lose control of the big Vega once and he probably wouldn't have been able to pull out of a deadly spin before plunging into the water. This is exactly what Denham Scott and Eddie Cooper felt happened. Frost probably lost control and suddenly the Vega was spinning wildly toward the water. Without a visible horizon even an experienced pilot would have trouble pulling out. Probably the Vega sank almost immediately. A small amount of debris and a spreading oil slick was all that remained of the beautiful bird. And even these traces were wiped out in a few moments.

16

RESULTS

The immediate effects of the Pacific Air Race, though not good, were certainly as expected. It appears from the vantage point of the 1980s that the popular reaction in late 1927 was to demand government controls on flying and to criticize Jim Dole and anyone else even remotely connected with the Pacific Air Race. Many people, who in May and June were grabbing headlines praising the organizers and participants in the race, were again grasping just as hard for headlines in September and October, trying to convince everyone that the Pacific Air Race was one of the biggest tragedies in the history of aviation. One of the first changes, as a result of the deaths suffered, was the way people referred to the race. Prior to its start it was almost always called the Pacific Air Race. Afterwards it became known as the Dole Race, the Dole Derby, or the Dole Tragedy. Apparently the public wanted to blame someone, and they chose Dole. If there was one man who should not be blamed directly it was Jim Dole.

True, Dole furnished the prizes, but he also offered cash rewards for anyone who could locate any of the downed fliers. He laid down the initial rules, but he deferred to the Department of Commerce experts in all matters concerning safety. He personally worked relentlessly and spent long hours with many people tracing tentative leads concerning the lost aircraft. But most of this was overlooked by the public.

Quite a few deaths are associated with the Pacific Air Race, but surely Dole could not be blamed for the deaths that occured prior to the race. The people who were unfortunate enough to lose their lives while preparing for the race were either ill-equipped or ill-prepared for their mission. Rules can only be made to cover minimum requirements. Adding a passenger and additional weight to the *Miss Doran* was asking for trouble, but none of the rules specifically stated that additional weight or people couldn't be carried. Many people tried to dissuade Mildred Doran from flying as a passenger but to no avail. All the government officials and the Navy advisors tried to stress the requirement for a capable navigator and insisted the person performing that function be at least able to handle standard dead reckoning and primary celestial navigation procedures. Through their efforts, at least a few incompetent people were eliminated. But many of the entrants treated this requirement as meaningless, as witness Bill Erwin's attempt to use his young wife as his navigator. The government experts had also strongly recommended, even in the initial rules, that radio equipment be carried; however, they did not make this an actual requirement, only a recommendation. Very few airplanes carried radios. A number of people had been lost in aircraft accidents in the years preceding the Pacific Air Race in various attempts to span the Atlantic, yet the critics completely ignored this fact. This was probably because the Atlantic deaths occurred one or two at a time rather than in a group, and they were spread over a longer period of time.

Many of the newspapers and magazine reports following the race bear quoting if for no other reason but to compare them to the reports before the race. They also demonstrate how fickle the public and the news media can be when they have the advantage of hindsight.

"Cut out the death dealing stunts" was a statement in the St. Louis *Star* editorial entitled "Dole's Race To Death," printed shortly after the race.

"Will somebody please explain what good purpose has been served by this competitive flight" asked the Brooklyn *Eagle*. The Boston *Post* referred to the race as "a mistake," while the Louisville *Times* used the terms "Aviation Asininity." The Winston Salem *Journal* asked "Was It Worth The Price—Ten Lives?" Many others echoed the same thoughts. In Norfolk, the *Virginia Pilot* probably summed it up well in its issue of 23 August, under the heading "Dole Derby Hindsight" as follows:

> The first trans-oceanic air race in history on the basis of present information figures up as follows: Four racers alive and victorious, three racers killed in the preliminaries, five racers missing for nearly a week and presumed dead, two racers missing four days and probably dead, value of prizes won $35,000 cost of race and value of machines lost, preparations for flight etc. more than $300,000, useful contribution to aeronautics—zero.

The same article went on to discuss Lindbergh and the tour that he was making throughout the United States at the time. They seriously criticized Lindbergh's travels and the fact that many cities were begging the extremely tired flier to visit. They went on to discuss the dirigible *Shenandoah*, which had crashed two years previously on 3 September 1925. They ended the article with "Hindsight but no foresight and no mercy."

Many supposedly learned people were quoted in statements that showed a lack of knowledge of aeronautics. Admiral Eberle demanded that the Navy abolish land planes for overwater flights. Secretary of the Navy Curtis D. Wilbur stated that the federal government should take moves to prevent recurrence of disasters such as those that befell the Dole race entries. All of the articles and statements had one thing in common; they stressed ten lives were lost. But none of them brought out the fact that only five were lost by actual bona fide contestants in the race and that even one of those was a passenger, Mildred Doran, who had absolutely no reason for being in the airplane.

The Philadelphia *Enquirer* flatly stated "Such an orgy of reckless sacrifice must never be permitted again in this country. Trans-Atlantic flights should be restricted to planes which are specially equipped for landing on the sea surface." This simplistic recommendation didn't even include both oceans, though its writer somehow thought using a seaplane would correct spins, disorientation in fog, overloading the airplane, lack of navigational ability, and lack of sufficient fuel to reach the destination.

A few small defensive voices could be heard. A Philadelphia *Public Ledger* editorial stated:

> It would be a bad thing to force regulation upon the courageous. It may be that had there been regulation Lindbergh would never have flown to glory. Some of the more splendid chapters of aviation might never have been written had authorities stood by when they were begun. Nevertheless ten lives gone in a single effort is a tremendous price to pay for a flight that could add little or nothing to the advance of flying. This cannot go on, the fliers must be protected from their own adventurous and danger loving selves. If regulation is the answer then regulation must come.

Assistant Secretary of Commerce William P. McCracken, Jr., government supervisor of commercial aviation, in an interview to United Press stated:

> Hawaiian flight is not nearly so bad as the fatal accidents caused by inexperienced aviators flying in this country without licenses. This latter must be stopped. . . . I deeply regret the loss of life in the Dole flight. I would not stop flights that are reasonable and practical, but I would see that they are carefully regulated.

The New York *Herald Tribune* voiced its opinion in a very profound editorial:

> One automatically begins to exclaim that there ought to be a law until one stops with the reflection that it would be a poorer world if man were not allowed to hazard his life and everyone were made a coward by legislative enactment. The motto "Better safe than sorry" though a sound work a day rule is not a noble principle for extraordinary occasions. Anxious publics pray for the rescue of these aviators only because they took the risk of not being rescued. If they had not been permitted to take the risk it would have mattered to few whether they lived or died. This is not cynicism. Were the emotions and the risks of adventure to be eliminated men and women would have approached the status of automatist. The reckless way of man belongs with his finest side.

M. E. Tracey in the Washington *News* wrote: "Worthwhile triumphs never have and never will come without risk." He further continued:

> Fatality has always dogged the trail of pioneers. A century and a half ago it was quite as dangerous to walk from Pittsburgh to Cleveland as it is to fly from New York to Paris now. The first year the Pilgrim fathers spent at Plymouth they lost more than half their number. Of the first 12,000 people who came to America two-thirds had perished within a decade. The time has not yet arrived when we can be safe and successful at the same time. This generation must dare and do like any other. Nothing has come into life to make it secure for those that lead the way. Humanity can stand still without taking chances, but cannot move forward.

No one, least of all James Dole, was happy about the way events turned out in the Pacific Air Race. But as some of the writers pointed out, progress has never been easy. Especially in the field of aviation, progress has always been costly in equipment, time, and lives. Realizing that less than twenty-four years had passed since a single man had made the first flight in history, which consisted of a 120-foot semi-controlled glide, makes the achievements of the Dole fliers better appreciated.

Six short years after the Dole race, on 1 August 1934, the first of three four-engine Sikorsky S–42 flying boats was test flown at Bridgeport, Connecticut. After a few months of test flying, one of the three, the *Pacific Clipper*, rose from San Francisco Bay in sight of the Oakland Airport, flew westward through the Golden Gate, and, 18 hours 9 minutes later, landed at Pearl Harbor, Hawaii. This was 16–17 April 1935. By November 1935, the Martin-built *China Clipper* was duplicating the feat, and by early 1936 scheduled passenger service was established from San Francisco to Manila by way of Hawaii. Surely the Dole contestants accomplished their purpose, for without their efforts and sacrifices Pacific aviation would surely have been delayed for many years.

As thousands of tourists and business people fly daily across the Pacific, many from the airport now known as Oakland International, one wonders how many give a thought to the flights of the *Woolaroc* and the *Aloha* that blazed the aerial trail. Art Goebel, Bill Davis, Marty Jensen, and Paul Schluter gambled and won. Others of the group of Dole race fliers were less lucky but no less brave. Many never received the accolades they deserved, and their sacrifices should never be forgotten.

George Covell, Richard Waggener, Arthur Rogers, Augy Pedlar, Vilas Knope, Jack Frost, Gordon Scott, Bill Erwin, Alvin Eichwoldt, and Mildred Doran. Any one or all of them could have waited nine short years and then bought a ticket to fly safely and routinely across the Pacific—but they didn't. They gambled and lost, but they paved the way for all the ticket holders who still owe them recognition and thanks.

Next time you're in a plane over the Pacific stop and think, "What's so great about flying to Hawaii? Is there any other way to go?"

APPENDIX:
AIRCRAFT SPECIFICATIONS

Aircraft Specifications

PLANE: ALOHA

TYPE: MODIFIED BREESE MONOPLANE
    HIGH WING
    CLOSED COCKPIT
    CLOSED CABIN

BUILDER: BREESE AIRCRAFT
    SAN FRANCISCO, CALIF.

CREW PILOT: MARTIN JENSEN
    HONOLULU, HAWAII

NAVIGATOR: PAUL SCHLUTER

SPONSOR: MARTIN JENSEN AND
    HAWAIIAN GROUP

STATISTICS:
    WING SPAN: 41 ft.
    WING AREA: 260 sq. ft.
    WING CHORD:
    LENGTH: 27 feet
    HEIGHT:
    WEIGHT: 4980 TAKEOFF. ALSO REPORTED 1500 MTY
                                               4300 TAKEOFF.
    FUEL CAP: 380 gals.
    TANKS: STANDARD WING AND INTERNAL FUSELAGE
    CONSTRUCTION: STEEL TUBE FUSELAGE FRAME. WOOD WING.
                      FABRIC COVERING. SINGLE WRIGHT J-5 ENGINE.

PERFORMANCE: SPEEDS: MAX: 110 mph   OTHER:
                      CRUISE: 84 mph
                      LANDING:

COLORING: YELLOW WITH
    RED DETAILS

MARKING: HAWAIIAN LEI AND
    SEAL OF TERRITORY
    OF HAWAII ON
    FUSELAGE. BLACK
    LETTERING "NX-914"
    ON WING AND TAIL.
    LARGE BLACK
    LETTERING ENTIRE
    SIDES OF FUSELAGE,
    "ALOHA."

EVENTUAL DISPOSITION: USED FOR CHARTER FLYING IN HAWAII AND
    LATER FOR NEWSPAPER FLYING IN UNITED
    STATES. DESTROYED IN HANGER FIRE,
    ROOSEVELT FIELD, N.Y.

REMARKS: ASSIGNED TAKEOFF NO. 11. ACTUAL TAKEOFF NO. 6.
    FINISHED SECOND IN RACE. TOTAL OF 6 CLOSED BREESE
    MONOPLANES BUILT IN 1927.

Aircraft Specifications

PLANE: ANGEL OF LOS ANGELES

TYPE: MID-WING MONOPLANE
TWIN ENGINE
OPEN COCKPIT

BUILDER: BRYANT
LOS ANGELES, CALIF.

CREW PILOT: ARTHUR V. ROGERS
LOS ANGELES, CALIF.

NAVIGATOR:

SPONSOR: LELAND A. BRYANT
LOS ANGELES, CALIF.

STATISTICS:
  WING SPAN:
  WING AREA: 340 sq. ft.
  WING CHORD:
  LENGTH:
  HEIGHT:
  WEIGHT:
  FUEL CAP: 408 gals.
  TANKS:
  CONSTRUCTION: TWO BRITISH LUCIFER RADIAL ENGINES, THREE CYLINDER, 467 CU. IN., 120 HORSEPOWER EACH, MOUNTED IN TANDEM. COCKPIT BETWEEN ENGINES. TWIN RUDDERS MOUNTED ON TAIL BOOMS.

PERFORMANCE: SPEEDS: MAX: *OTHER:*
              CRUISE:
              LANDING:

COLORING: *MARKING:* "NX–705"

EVENTUAL DISPOSITON:

REMARKS: ASSIGNED TAKEOFF NO. 14. CRASHED ON TAKEOFF ON TEST FLIGHT. ARTHUR ROGERS KILLED.

Aircraft Specifications

PLANE: CITY OF PEORIA

TYPE: BIPLANE
OPEN COCKPIT
TWO PLACE

BUILDER: AIR KING
NATIONAL
AIRWAYS SYSTEM
LOMAX, ILL.

CREW PILOT: CHARLIE W. PARKHURST
PEORIA, ILL.

NAVIGATOR: RALPH C. LOWES, JR.

SPONSOR: NATIONAL AIRWAYS
SYSTEM
LOMAX, ILL.

STATISTICS:
WING SPAN: Upper 34 ft. 2 in.
Lower 37 ft. 6 in. approx.
WING AREA: 342 sq. ft.
WING CHORD: 61.5 in.
LENGTH:
HEIGHT:
WEIGHT: Reported 4500 lbs.
FUEL CAP: 368 gals.
TANKS: TOTAL OF FOUR, FORWARD FUSELAGE SECTION
CONSTRUCTION: STEEL TUBE FUSELAGE FRAME. WOOD WINGS.
FABRIC COVERING. SINGLE WRIGHT J–5 ENGINE.

PERFORMANCE: SPEEDS: MAX:
CRUISE: 85 to 90 mph
LANDING:
OTHER: 14 sec. takeoff at one-half load.

COLORING: WHITE FUSELAGE
(possibly silver)
BLUE NOSE
BLUE STRIPE,
TOP OF
FUSELAGE

MARKING: ALL LETTERING BLACK: "NX–3070" ON WINGS AND TAIL. "AIR KING" ON VERTICAL FIN AND FUSELAGE SIDES. "C.W. PARKHURST, PILOT/R.C. LOWES JR. NAVIGATOR" ON FUSELAGE SIDES. "MANUFACTURED AND OWNED BY NATIONAL AIRWAYS SYSTEM LOMAX, ILLINOIS" ON FUSELAGE SIDES, REAR.

EVENTUAL DISPOSITION: RETURNED TO LOMAX, ILL., AFTER RACE.
ENGINE LATER USED IN AIR KING "MONO FOUR."

REMARKS: ASSIGNED TAKEOFF NO. 3. DISQUALIFIED FOR LACK OF FUEL ONE HOUR BEFORE RACE START. USED STANDARD RED CROWN FUEL. TOTAL OF 55 AIR KINGS (OX–5 ENGINE) BUILT IN 1927.

Aircraft Specifications

PLANE: DALLAS SPIRIT

TYPE: HIGH-WING MONOPLANE
  CLOSED COCKPIT
  CLOSED CABIN

BUILDER: COPIED FROM SWALLOW

STATISTICS:
  WING SPAN: 48 ft.
  WING AREA: 330 sq. ft.
  WING CHORD:
  LENGTH: 30 1/2 ft.
  HEIGHT:
  WEIGHT: 5650 lbs. TAKEOFF
  FUEL CAP: 480 gals.
  TANKS: FUSELAGE AND WING
  CONSTRUCTION: STEEL TUBE FUSELAGE FRAME. WOOD WING. FABRIC COVERING. SINGLE WRIGHT J–5 ENGINE.

CREW PILOT: WILLIAM P. ERWIN

NAVIGATOR: ALVIN H. EICHWOLDT

SPONSOR: DALLAS, TEXAS, GROUP PHILLIPS OIL CO. FUEL.

PERFORMANCE: SPEEDS: MAX: 126 mph   *OTHER*:
  CRUISE: 105 mph
  LANDING: 45 mph

COLORING: DARK GREEN FUSELAGE SILVER WING AND TAIL. HAS ALSO BEEN LISTED AS BLUE FUSELAGE AND WHITE WING.

MARKING: BLACK LETTERING "NX–941" ON WING AND TAIL. "DALLAS SPIRIT" IN LARGE WHITE LETTERS BOTH SIDES OF FUSELAGE.

EVENTUAL DISPOSITION: TOOK OFF TWO DAYS AFTER RACE FOR HAWAII. LOST AT SEA.

REMARKS: ASSIGNED TAKEOFF NO. 5. ACTUAL TAKEOFF NO. 8. RETURNED AFTER TAKEOFF WITH FABRIC RIPPED ON REAR AND BOTTOM OF FUSELAGE. SWALLOW CO. BUILT ONLY 1 CLOSED MONOPLANE (J–5 ENGINE) IN 1927.

PLANE: DETROIT MESSENGER *CREW PILOT:* FRED A. GILES

TYPE: HESS MODEL BLUEBIRD
   BIPLANE

NAVIGATOR:

BUILDER: HESS AIRCRAFT
   WYANDOTTE,   *SPONSOR:*
   MICH.

STATISTICS:
   WING SPAN:
   WING AREA: 295 sq. ft.
   WING CHORD:
   LENGTH:
   HEIGHT:
   FUEL CAP: 500 gals.
   CONSTRUCTION: SINGLE WRIGHT J–5 ENGINE.

PERFORMANCE: SPEEDS: MAX: *OTHER:*
   CRUISE:
   LANDING:

COLORING: *MARKING:*

EVENTUAL DISPOSITION: FLOWN TO OAKLAND FEW DAYS AFTER RACE. USED BY CAPT. GILES IN NOV. 1927 IN ATTEMPT TO CROSS PACIFIC. RETURNED TO SAN FRANCISCO AFTER FEW HOURS.

REMARKS: ASSIGNED TAKEOFF NO. 6. DID NOT ARRIVE IN OAKLAND IN TIME FOR RACE.

Aircraft Specifications

PLANE: EL ENCANTO

TYPE: MODIFIED GODDARD
SPORT PLANE
HIGH-WING MONOPLANE
CLOSED COCKPIT
TANDEM SEATING

BUILDER: N. A. GODDARD

STATISTICS:
  WING SPAN: 42 ft.
  WING AREA: 283 1/2 sq. ft.
  WING CHORD:
  LENGTH:
  HEIGHT:
  WEIGHT:
  FUEL CAP: 360 gals.
  TANKS: STANDARD WING PLUS EXTERNAL BELLY TANK
  CONSTRUCTION: STEEL TUBE FUSELAGE FRAME. WOOD WING. FABRIC COVERING. SINGLE WRIGHT J-5 ENGINE.

PERFORMANCE: SPEEDS: MAX:
  CRUISE:
  LANDING:

COLORING: ALL SILVER

CREW PILOT: LT. NORM GODDARD, USNR
SAN DIEGO, CALIF.

NAVIGATOR: LT. KENNETH C. HAWKINS, USN
SAN DIEGO, CALIF.

SPONSOR: NORM. A. GODDARD
SAN DIEGO, CALIF.

OTHER:

MARKING: ALL LETTERING BLACK: "NX-5074" ON WING AND TAIL. "HBH" AND "DESIGNED AND BUILT BY NORMAN A. GODDARD SAN DIEGO, CA." ON VERTICAL FIN. "EL ENCANTO" DIAGONALLY ON COWLING.

EVENTUAL DISPOSITION: REPORTED REPAIRED AFTER RACE AT SAN LEANDRO, CALIF. LATER REBUILT BY GODDARD AT PALO ALTO, CALIF. NAMED THE "GYPSY."

REMARKS: "HBH" ON FIN STOOD FOR "HELL BENT FOR HONOLULU." ASSIGNED TAKEOFF NO. 2. ACTUAL TAKEOFF NO. 2. CRASHED ON TAKEOFF.

Aircraft Specifications

PLANE: GOLDEN EAGLE

TYPE: VEGA
   HIGH-WING MONOPLANE
   OPEN COCKPIT
   CLOSED CABIN

BUILDER: LOCKHEED AIRCRAFT CO.
   LOS ANGELES, CALIF.

CREW PILOT: JOHN W. FROST

NAVIGATOR: GORDON SCOTT

SPONSOR: GEORGE W. HEARST JR.
   SAN FRANCISCO, CALIF.

STATISTICS:
   WING SPAN: 41 ft.
   WING AREA: 260 sq. ft.
   WING CHORD:
   LENGTH: 27 ft. 6 in.
   HEIGHT:
   WEIGHT: 1750 MTY.
       4650 TAKEOFF
   FUEL CAP: 350 gals.
   TANKS: TWO FUSELAGE TANKS
       TWO 50 gal. WING TANKS.
   CONSTRUCTION: MOLDED PLYWOOD SEMI-MONOCOQUE FUSELAGE.
       WOOD WING. PLYWOOD COVERING.
       SINGLE WRIGHT J–5 ENGINE, SER. NO. 7550

PERFORMANCE: SPEEDS: MAX: 135 mph   OTHER: 3,500-mile RANGE
       CRUISE: 118 mph
       LANDING: 49 mph

COLORING: ORANGE WITH
   RED TRIM

MARKING: BLACK LETTERING. "NX–913" ON WING AND TAIL. LOCKHEED STAR TRADEMARK ON FIN. NAME "GOLDEN EAGLE" IN SMALL LETTERS BOTH SIDES OF FUSELAGE.

EVENTUAL DISPOSITION: APPARENTLY LOST AT SEA

REMARKS: ASSIGNED TAKEOFF NO. 15. ACTUAL TAKEOFF NO. 4. DISAPPEARED OVER PACIFIC. ORIGINAL REG. NO. 2788 CHANGED BEFORE RACE. PROTOTYPE OF LATER LINE OF LOCKHEED VEGAS.

Aircraft Specifications

PLANE: HUMMINGBIRD

TYPE: LOW-WING MONOPLANE
    CLOSED COCKPIT
    CLOSED CABIN

BUILDER: TREMAINE

STATISTICS:
    WING SPAN:
    WING AREA:
    WING CHORD:
    LENGTH:
    HEIGHT:
    FUEL CAP:
    CONSTRUCTION:

CREW PILOT: LT. GEORGE W. D. COVELL, USN

NAVIGATOR: LT. RICHARD S. WAGGENER, USN

SPONSOR: W. D. TREMAINE
    FRED W. BURGH
    DR. CLAUDE BURSON

PERFORMANCE: SPEEDS: MAX:
                  CRUISE:
                  LANDING:

OTHER:

COLORING: MARKING:

EVENTUAL DISPOSITION:

REMARKS: ASSIGNED TAKEOFF NO. 13. CRASHED ON TAKEOFF AT SAN DIEGO ENROUTE TO OAKLAND. LTS. G. COVELL AND R. WAGGENER KILLED.

Aircraft Specifications

PLANE: MISS DORAN

TYPE: MODIFIED BUHL CA–5
    AIR SEDAN
    BIPLANE
    CLOSED COCKPIT
    CLOSED CABIN

BUILDER: BUHL AIRCRAFT
    MARYSVILLE,
    MICH.

CREW PILOT: JOHN A. PEDLAR

NAVIGATOR: LT. VILAS R. KNOPE, USN

PASSENGER: MILDRED DORAN

SPONSOR: WILLIAM MALLOSKA
    LINCOLN PETROLEUM
    CO. FLINT, MICH.

STATISTICS:
  WING SPAN: 42 ft.
  WING AREA: 350 sq. ft.
  WING CHORD:
  LENGTH:
  HEIGHT:
  WEIGHT: PROBABLY OVER 5000
        REPORTED 2100 MTY. 4980 TAKEOFF.
  FUEL CAP: 400 gals.
  TANKS: FUSELAGE AND WING
  CONSTRUCTION: STEEL TUBE FUSELAGE FRAME. WOOD WINGS.
        FABRIC COVERING. SINGLE WRIGHT J–5 ENGINE.

PERFORMANCE: *SPEEDS*: MAX: 118 mph   *OTHER*: STD. CA–5
                      CRUISE: 100 mph   MAX. 120 mph
                      LANDING: 48 mph   CRUISE 105 mph

COLORING: RED WINGS
    AND NOSE
    WHITE FUSELAGE
    BLUE TAIL

MARKING: BLACK LETTERING:
    "NX–2915" ON WINGS
    AND TAIL. "LINCOLN
    OILS LPCo FLINT, MI."
    LOGO ON BOTH SIDES.
    "MISS DORAN FLINT.,
    MI. " IN SEMICIRCLE
    AROUND LOWER HALF
    OF COWLING.

EVENTUAL DISPOSITION: LOST AT SEA DURING RACE.

REMARKS: ASSIGNED TAKEOFF NO. 4. ACTUAL TAKE OFF NO. 5.
        RETURNED WITH FOULED PLUGS. TOOK OFF AGAIN AFTER
        REPAIRS. TOTAL OF 8 BUHL CA–5s BUILT IN 1927.

Aircraft Specifications

PLANE: MISS HOLLYDALE

TYPE: INTERNATIONAL F-17-W BIPLANE OPEN COCKPIT

BUILDER: INTERNATIONAL AIRCRAFT CO. LONG BEACH, CALIF.

CREW PILOT: FRANK CLARK

NAVIGATOR: JEFF WARREN

SPONSOR: CHARLIE BABB
LOS ANGELES, CALIF.

E. A. PARKFORD
LOS ANGELES, CALIF.

STATISTICS:
WING SPAN: UPPER 35 ft.
LOWER 35 ft.
WING AREA: 325 sq. ft.
WING CHORD:
LENGTH: 24 ft. 6 in.
HEIGHT: 9 ft. 6 in.
WEIGHT:
FUEL CAP: 400 gals.
TANKS:
CONSTRUCTION:

PERFORMANCE: SPEEDS: MAX: 130 mph   OTHER:
CRUISE: 110 mph
LANDING: 42 mph

COLORING: BLACK FUSELAGE ORANGE WINGS AND TAIL

MARKING: WHITE LETTERING ON FUSELAGE "MISS HOLLYDALE" BOTH SIDES. BLACK LETTERING ON WINGS AND TAIL.

EVENTUAL DISPOSITION: WAS PROTOTYPE FOR 1929 VERSION OF INTERNATIONAL F-17-W. PROBABLY REBUILT AS STANDARD F-17-W AFTER RACE.

REMARKS: ASSIGNED TAKEOFF NO. 12. WITHDREW BEFORE RACE. NOTE: SPEEDS AND DIMENSIONS SHOWN ARE FOR STANDARD F-17-W. TOTAL OF 32 OPEN COCKPIT OX-5 POWERED INTERNATIONALS BUILT IN 1927.

Aircraft Specifications

PLANE: OKLAHOMA

TYPE: MODIFIED TRAVEL AIR 5000 HIGH-WING MONOPLANE CLOSED FIVE-PLACE CABIN

BUILDER: TRAVEL AIR CO. WICHITA, KANS.

STATISTICS:
 WING SPAN: 50 ft. 4 1/2 in.
 WING AREA: 310 sq. ft.
 WING CHORD:
 LENGTH: 31 ft. 2 in.
 HEIGHT: 7 ft. 3 1/2 in.
 WEIGHT: 2200 MTY.
  5200 TAKEOFF.
 FUEL CAP: 425 gals.
 TANKS: INTERNAL FUSELAGE AND WING
 CONSTRUCTION: STEEL TUBE FUSELAGE FRAME. WOOD WING. FABRIC COVERING. SINGLE WRIGHT J–5 ENGINE

PERFORMANCE: SPEEDS: MAX:
  CRUISE:
  LANDING:

COLORING: TRAVEL AIR BLUE FUSELAGE. TRAVEL AIR YELLOW WING.

CREW PILOT: BENNY GRIFFIN BARTLESVILLE, OKLA.

NAVIGATOR: AL HENLEY BARTLESVILLE, OKLA.

SPONSOR: GEORGE HENSHAW OKLAHOMA CITY, OKLA.

PHILLIPS OIL CO. BARTLESVILLE, OKLA.

OTHER:

MARKING: WHITE LETTERING ON FUSELAGE, "OKLAHOMA." BLACK "NX–911" ON WINGS AND TAIL. SQUARE EMBLEM LOCATED ON FUSELAGE BELOW WING WORDED "PHILLIPS NU-AVIATION GASOLINE."

EVENTUAL DISPOSITION: ALL CYLINDERS REPLACED ON ENGINE AFTER RACE. SOLD TO ERIN GREENLEAF AND DAN SAUDER, OPERATORS OF A BUS LINE IN WICHITA, KANS. USED FOR SOME EXHIBITON FLYING AND FEW LONG DISTANCE RECORD ATTEMPTS.

REMARKS: ASSIGNED TAKEOFF NO. 1. ACTUAL TAKEOFF NO. 1. RETURNED WITH BURNED-OUT ENGINE. LANDED SAFELY, OUT OF RACE. TOTAL OF 14 T/A 5000s BUILT IN 1927.

Aircraft Specifications

PLANE: PABCO PACIFIC FLYER   *CREW PILOT*: LIVINGSTON G. IRVING

TYPE: HIGH-WING MONOPLANE
    CLOSED COCKPIT
    CLOSED CABIN   *NAVIGATOR*:

BUILDER: BREESE AIRCRAFT   PARAFFIN CO.
    SAN FRANCISCO, CALIF.   *SPONSOR*: BERKELEY, CALIF.

STATISTICS:
  WING SPAN: 41 ft.
  WING AREA: 260 sq. ft.
  WING CHORD:
  LENGTH: 27 feet
  HEIGHT:
  WEIGHT: OVER 5000 LBS. ALSO REPORTED 4300 TAKEOFF
                                                      1500 MTY.
  FUEL CAP: 380 gals.
  TANKS: TWO 150 gal. IN FUSELAGE
    TWO 40 gal. IN WING
  CONSTRUCTION: STEEL TUBE FUSELAGE FRAME. WOOD WING.
    FABRIC COVERING. SINGLE WRIGHT J–5 ENGINE.

PERFORMANCE: *SPEEDS*: *MAX*: 110 mph   *OTHER*: ALSO LISTED AS 100–
                CRUISE: 84 mph   115 CRUISE SPEED AND
                LANDING: 3500 MILE RANGE.

COLORING: ORANGE WING   *MARKING*: BLACK LETERING ON
    BLACK FUSELAGE   WING WHITE
                                             LETTERING
                                             REMAINDER "NX–646"
                                             ON WING AND TAIL.

EVENTUAL DISPOSITION:

REMARKS: ASSIGNED TAKEOFF NO. 7. ACTUAL TAKEOFF NO. 3. CRASHED
    ON TAKEOFF. TOTAL OF 6 BREESE MONOPLANES BUILT IN
      1927.

Aircraft Specifications

PLANE: PRIDE OF LOS ANGELES

CREW PILOT: JAMES A. GIFFIN

TYPE: MODIFIED FISK CF–10
TRIPLANE
TWIN ENGINE
OPEN COCKPIT
CLOSED CABIN

NAVIGATOR: TEN LUNDGREN

SPONSOR: HOOT GIBSON
HOLLYWOOD, CALIF.

BUILDER: INTERNATIONAL CO.

STATISTICS:
WING SPAN: 45 ft.
WING AREA:
WING CHORD:
LENGTH:
HEIGHT:
TANKS:
CONSTRUCTION: STANDARD STEEL TUBE FUSELAGE FRAME. WOOD WINGS. FABRIC COVERING. TWO WRIGHT J–5 ENGINES.

PERFORMANCE: SPEEDS: MAX: .
CRUISE:
LANDING:

OTHER:

COLORING: PROBABLY ALL BLACK

MARKING:

EVENTUAL DISPOSITION: CRASHED, DAMAGED BEYOND REPAIR BEFORE RACE AT OAKLAND

REMARKS: ASSIGNED TAKEOFF NO. 8. CRASHED ON LANDING AT OAKLAND. NO FATALITIES, PLANE DEMOLISHED.

Aircraft Specifications

PLANE: WOOLAROC

TYPE: MODIFIED TRAVEL AIR 5000 HIGH-WING MONOPLANE CLOSED FIVE-PLACE CABIN

BUILDER: TRAVEL AIR CO. WICHITA, KANS.

STATISTICS:
  WING SPAN: 50 ft. 4 1/2 in.
  WING AREA: 310 sq. ft.
  WING CHORD:
  LENGTH: 31 ft. 2 in.
  HEIGHT: 7 ft. 3 1/2 in.
  WEIGHT: 2200 MTY
      5200 TAKEOFF.
  FUEL CAP: 425 gals.
  TANKS: INTERNATIONAL FUSELAGE AND WING
  CONSTRUCTION: STEEL TUBE FUSELAGE FRAME. WOOD WING. FABRIC COVERING. SINGLE WRIGHT J-5 ENGINE.

CREW PILOT: ART GOEBEL

NAVIGATOR: LT. WILLIAM V. DAVIS, JR., USN

SPONSOR: ART GOEBEL AND GROUP OF FRIENDS

PHILLIPS OIL CO. BARTLESVILLE, OKLA.

PERFORMANCE: SPEEDS: MAX:
       CRUISE:
       LANDING:

OTHER:

COLORING: TRAVEL AIR BLUE FUSELAGE. TRAVEL AIR YELLOW WING.

MARKING: WHITE LETTERING ON FUSELAGE "WOOLAROC." BLACK "NX-869" ON WING AND TAIL. DIAGONAL DRIFT LINES ON TOP OF FUSELAGE AND TAIL.

EVENTUAL DISPOSITION: LATER USED BY GOEBEL FOR DEMONSTRATION FLIGHTS AROUND UNITED STATES. BOUGHT BACK BY FRANK PHILLIPS AND PLACED ON DISPLAY AT WOOLAROC MUSEUM,. BARTLESVILLE, OKLA. STILL ON DISPLAY.

REMARKS: ASSIGNED TAKEOFF NO. 9. ACTUAL TAKEOFF NO. 7. FINISHED FIRST IN RACE. TOTAL OF 14 T/A 5000s BUILT IN 1927.

NOTES

CHAPTER 1

Published sources for Chapter 1 include Richard K. Smith's *First Across*, Charles A. Lindbergh's *We*, Lowell Thomas's *The First World Flight*, *United States Naval Aviation, 1910-1970*, the *Aircraft Yearbook* of 1919 and 1920, and the Honolulu *Star Bulletin* of 25 May 1927. Additional sources include telegrams and data of the Dole Company supplied by Castle & Cooke Inc.

CHAPTER 2

Sources for Chapter 2 include the maintenance manual for the Wright J–5 engine, the Honolulu *Advertiser* of 22 June 1927, and the Honolulu *Star Bulletin* of 25 May, 27 May, 12 July, 13 July, and 16 August 1927. Unpublished sources include copies of Dole Company telegrams supplied by Castle & Cooke Inc. Additional personal information came from E. Leigh Stevens of the Dole Company through interviews and correspondence with R. Scheppler.

CHAPTER 3

Published sources for Chapter 3 include Edward Jablonski's *Sea Wings*, William J. Horrat's *Above the Pacific*, Dick Grace's *Visibility Unlimited* and his *Squadron of Death*, E. J. Millikan's article on Grace in the *American Aviation Historical Society Journal*, and the *Aircraft Year Book* of 1928. Useful newspapers include the Honolulu *Advertiser* of 22 June, 29 June, and 12 July 1927; the Honolulu *Star Bulletin* of 22 June, 27 June, and 30 June 1927; and the San Francisco *Chronicle* of 14 July 1927. Additional data was supplied by Eddie Cooper and Lester Maitland through interviews with R. Scheppler.

CHAPTER 4

Sources for Chapter 4 include *United States Naval Aviation, 1910-1970*, and the Honolulu *Advertiser* of 29 June 1927. Rules and entry requirements were supplied by Eddie Cooper.

CHAPTER 5

Published sources for Chapter 5 include Richard Sanders Allen's *Revolution in the Sky*, Joseph P. Juptner's *U.S. Civil Aircraft*, Ed Phillips's *Travel Air*, and the *Aircraft Year Book* of 1928. Relevant articles include Paul D. Stevens's "The Air Kings of Lomax," Helen M. Scheetz's "Glenn Romkey and the Air King," and "To Wichita in 15 Hours" in the July 1927 issue of *Western Flying*. Further details were found in Lockheed Aircraft Corporation's *Days of Trial and Triumph*, Beech Aircraft Company brochures and literature, National Airways System literature, a Hess Aircraft Company brochure reprinted in the November 1958 issue of *American Airman*, and "Fisk Tri-Plane Details" in *Aero Digest* of July 1931. Newspaper sources include the Honolulu *Advertiser* of 10 August 1927, the Honolulu *Star Bulletin* of 9 August and 18 August 1927, and the Peoria *Journal* of 20 July, 27 July, and 4–14 August 1927. Considerable information was supplied through interviews and personal files of Billy Parker, Benny Griffin, Ken Boedecker, Marty Jensen, Jerome Lederer, Jack Romkey, Eddie Cooper, and Denham Scott.

CHAPTER 6

Newspaper sources for Chapter 6 include the Honolulu *Advertiser* of 10 August, 15 August, and 17 August 1927 and the Honolulu *Star Bulletin* of 13 August and 16 August 1927. Additional information was obtained from Billy Parker, Eddie Cooper, Marty Jensen, and Jack Romkey through interviews and correspondence with R. Scheppler.

CHAPTER 7

Sources for Chapter 7 include the Honolulu *Advertiser* of 10 August and 15 August 1927; the Honolulu *Star Bulletin* of 9 August, 13 August, and 16 August 1927; and the Oakland *Tribune* of 15 August 1927.

CHAPTER 8

Newspaper sources for Chapter 8 include the Brooklyn *Eagle* of 16 August 1927, the Honolulu *Star Bulletin* of 13 August and 16 August 1927, and the San Francisco *Chronicle* of 16 August and 17 August 1927. Additional information was obtained through personal file data, correspondence, and interviews with Billy Parker, Denham Scott, Eddie Cooper, Jack Romkey, Ken Boedecker, Benny Griffin, and Marty Jensen.

CHAPTER 9

Newspaper sources for Chapter 9 include the Brooklyn *Eagle* of 16 August 1927, the Honolulu *Advertiser* of 17 August 1927, the Honolulu *Star Bulletin* of 16 August and 17 August 1927, the Oakland *Tribune* of 17 August 1927, the Peoria *Journal* of 16 August 1927, and the San Francisco *Chronicle* of 16 August 1927. Additional information was obtained through personal interviews with Eddie Cooper, Marty Jensen, Benny Griffin, and Billy Parker.

CHAPTER 10

Sources for Chapter 10 include the Honolulu *Advertiser* of 18 August 1927, the Honolulu *Star Bulletin* of 16 August and 18 August 1927, and the Oakland *Tribune* of 17 August 1927.

CHAPTER 11

Published sources for Chapter 11 include Martin Jensen's article "Aloha" in *Sport Aviation* of June 1967 and the newspapers Honolulu *Advertiser* of 18 August 1927 and 19 May 1982 and Honolulu *Star Bulletin* of 18 August 1927 and 9 August 1952. Additional information was obtained through personal interviews with Martin Jensen.

CHAPTER 12

Newspaper sources for Chapter 12 include the Honolulu *Star Bulletin* of 13 August and 16 August 1927; the Peoria *Journal* of 10 August, 14 August, 16 August, 19 August, 22 August, and 25 August 1927; and the San Francisco *Chronicle* of 16 August 1927. Relevant articles include Paul D. Stevens's "The Air Kings of Lomax" and Helen M. Scheetz's "Glenn Romkey and the Air King." Considerable data came from personal files and interviews with Jack Romkey.

CHAPTER 13

Newspaper sources for Chapter 13 include the Honolulu *Advertiser* of 18 August, 19 August, and 22 August 1927; the Honolulu *Star Bulletin* of 18 August 1927; and the San Francisco *Examiner* of 17 August and 19 August 1927. Additional information came from interviews with Denham Scott.

CHAPTER 14

Newspaper sources for Chapter 14 include the San Francisco *Call* of 20 August 1927 and the San Francisco *Examiner* of 19 August 1927. Additional information was obtained from interviews with Billy Parker and Marty Jensen.

CHAPTER 15

Published sources for Chapter 15 include Richard Sanders Allen's *Revolution in the Sky* and Al Slump's "The Great Airplane Massacre." Additional information was obtained from interviews with Denham Scott, Marty Jensen, and Eddie Cooper.

CHAPTER 16

Sources for Chapter 16 include the San Francisco *Examiner* of 19 August 1927, the *Weekly Times* of 3 September 1927, and "The Transpacific Air Derby" in *Literary Digest* of 27 August 1927. Other data came from correspondence of Kathleen Scott to James Dole and E. Leigh Stevens to R. Scheppler.

SELECT BIBLIOGRAPHY

BOOKS

Aircraft Year Book. Aeronautical Chamber of Commerce of America, 1919, 1920, 1928.
Allen, Richard Sanders. *Revolution in the Sky.* Stephen Green Press, 1964.
American Heritage History of Flight. American Heritage Publishing Co.,1962.
Days of Trial and Triumph. Lockheed Aircraft Corp., 1969.
Grace, Dick. *Visibility Unlimited.* Longsmans Green and Co., 1950.
———. *Squadron of Death.* Sun Dial Press, 1937.
Horrat, William J. *Above the Pacific.* Aero Publishers, 1966.
Jablonski, Edward. *Sea Wings.* Doubleday and Co., 1972.
Juptner, Joseph P. *U.S. Civil Aircraft.* Aero Publishers, 1962-80.
Lindbergh, Charles A. *We.* G. P. Putnam Sons, 1927.
Phillips, Ed. *Travel Air.* Flying Books, 1982.
Smith, Richard K. *First Across.* Naval Institute Press, 1973.
Thomas, Lowell. *The First World Flight.* Houghton Mifflin Co., 1925.
United States Naval Aviation, 1910-1970. NAVAIR 00-80P-1. U.S. Government Printing Office, 1970.
Welmana, A. Shrader. *Fifty Years of Flight.* Eaton Manufacturing Co., 1953.
Wright J–5 Engine Manual. Wright Aeronautical Corp., 1927

ARTICLES

"Counting the Cost of Stunt Flying." *Literary Digest* (27 Aug. 1927).
Editorials. *The Outlook* (31 Aug. 1927).
"Fisk Tri-Plane Details." *Aero Digest* (Sept. 1931).
Forden, L. N. "The Dole Race." *American Aviation Historical Society Journal* 20, no. 3 (1975).

Hess Aircraft Company brochure. Reprinted in *American Airman* (Nov. 1958).
Jensen, Martin. "Aloha." *Sport Aviation* (June 1967).
Kennedy, Hugh A. Studdert. "The Dole Race to Hawaii." *Outlook* (24 Aug. 1927).
Millikan, E. J. "Dick Grace and His Waterhouse Cruzair." *American Aviation Historical Society Journal* 24, no. 2 (1979).
Scheetz, Helen M. "Glenn Romkey and the Air King." *Antique Airplane News* (Jan. 1962).
Slump, Al. "The Great Airplane Massacre." *True Magazine* (1959).
Stevens, Paul D. "The Air Kings of Lomax." *American Aviation Historical Society Journal*.
"To Wichita in 15 Hours." *Western Flying* (July 1927).
"The Transpacific Air Derby." *Literary Digest* (27 Aug. 1927).
Travel Air Aircraft Company brochure. 1927.

NEWSPAPERS

Brooklyn *Eagle*. 16 Aug. 1927.
Honolulu *Advertiser*. 22 and 29 June, 12 and 13 July, 10, 15, 17, 18, 19, 22, 23, 24, and 30 Aug. 1927; 19 May 1982.
Honolulu *Star Bulletin*. 25 and 27 May, 22, 27, and 30 June, 9, 13, 16, 17, 18, 22, and 25 Aug 1927; 9 Aug. 1952.
Los Angeles *Evening Herald*. 29 June 1927.
Oakland *Tribune*. 15 and 17 Aug. 1927.
Peoria *Journal*. 20 July, 4, 5, 8, 9, 10, 14, 16, 19, 22, and 25 Aug. 1927.
San Francisco *Bulletin*. 14 Sept. 1927.
San Francisco *Call*. 20 Aug. 1927.
San Francisco *Chronicle*. 16 and 17 Aug. 1927; 14 July 1952.
San Francisco *Examiner*. 17 and 19 Aug. 1927.
San Francisco *Morning Post*. 22 Aug. 1927.

PERSONAL CONTACTS

Budwig, Gilbert	Early Lockheed employee. Correspondence.
Boedecker, Ken 1974	Wright Aeronautical Co. representative. Correspondence and phone interviews.
Cooper, Eddie 1967–78	Mechanic on *Golden Eagle*. Extensive interviews and use of complete newspaper and data files.

Griffin, Benny 1977 — Pilot of *Oklahoma*. Correspondence, phone interviews, and use of data files.

Jensen, Martin 1975–77 — Pilot of *Aloha*, second place winner. Correspondence, extensive interviews, and use of data files.

Kalina, Tim 1975 — Aero historian. Correspondence.

Lederer, Jerome — Engineer, Air King Co. Interview.

Maitland, Lester 1967 — Copilot of Army flight, first Pacific crossing. Interview.

Parker, Billy 1975–79 — Official of Phillips Oil Co. Extensive interviews and data files.

Plehinger, Russ 1972 — Aero historian. File data, photos.

Romkey, Jack 1977 — Son of Glenn Romkey, engineer and pilot, Air King Co. Extensive interviews and use of very complete data files of Air King Co. and Glenn Romkey.

Scott, Denham 1974–77 — Brother of Gordon Scott, navigator of *Golden Eagle*. Interviews and use of detailed files.

Stevens, E. Leigh 1974–75 — Assistant secretary of Castle and Cooke Inc., successor to Dole Co., and personal friend of James D. Dole. Interviews and complete use of Dole Co. files.

INDEX

Alcock, Capt. John 5
Alfara, Heraclio 35
Allen, Riley 6–7, 67
Arnold, C. N. 12

Babb, C. E. Charlie 47, 59, 61
Barkin, Walter F. 96
Barnes, K. B. 23
Barnholt, Charles 59
Beech, Walter 44–45, 69
Bellande, Edward 51, 52
Bishop, Billy 8
Bleriot, Louis Jr. 10
Block, Capt. Elmer 114
Boedecker, Ken 32, 69, 72, 77
Boyer, Frank O. 23
Breese, Lt. James 4
Breingan, Bill 55
Breinger, C. W. 96
Bronte, Emory 18, 20–21, 22, 85
Brown, Lt. Arthur W. 5
Brown, R. C. 12
Broyle, Bill 17
Bryant, Leland A. 50
Budwig, Gilbert 51
Burgh, Fred W. 49
Byrd, Cmdr. Richard 10, 100

Carter, Charles H. 16–18, 30
Chamberlain, Clarence 10, 16

Chandler, Cal 43
Chandler, H. 24
Clark, Clarence 32, 45
Clark, Frank 26, 29, 43, 47–48, 54, 55, 59, 61
Coli, Francis 6
Connell, Lt. Byron 5
Cooke, Clarence H. 12, 23
Cooke, T. A. 23
Cooper, Eddie 16–17, 20, 29, 51, 53, 56, 62, 73, 75–76, 114, 115, 116
Cooper, Mrs. Eddie 62
Covell, Lt. George W. D. 25, 29, 48–49, 56, 120
Covell, Mrs. George 56
Cummings, Chet 34

Davis, Bill 81–85, 88–90, 120
Davis, Lt. Cmdr. Noel 6
Dealey, E. M. 106, 108
Dodge, Col. Grant E. 19
Dole, James D. 3, 6–15, 20, 23–25, 29, 46, 58, 61, 64, 65, 66, 92–93, 102, 104, 117, 120
Donaldson, William H. 4
Doran, Mildred 28, 37–39, 60, 62, 63, 71, 72, 76, 78–79, 86, 104, 118, 119, 120
Dougherty, Earl 38, 46

Easterwood, William E. 39
Eberle, Adm. 118–119
Eichwoldt, Lt. Cmdr. Alvin H. 18, 61, 105, 106–110, 120
Erwin, Capt. William P. 16, 25, 28, 29, 39–40, 54, 55–57, 60, 61, 62, 70, 76, 78, 105, 106–110, 118, 120
Erwin, Mrs. William P. 28, 40, 56, 57, 61, 118

Fairbanks, Doug 8
Farrington, Joe 6–7, 67
Farrington, Gov. Wallace R. 12, 66, 91
Flenning, Dave 103
Flynn, C. A. 25
Fonck, Rene 6, 16
Ford, Alfred 4
Foss 103
Fowler, Robert 26, 29, 45, 54, 100, 101
Frost, John W. 25, 29, 44, 52–53, 55, 56, 62, 70, 73, 75, 82, 83, 87, 113–116, 120

Garrett, W. R. 25
Gephardt, V. 23–24
Gibson, Hoot 42
Giffin, Capt. James L. 26, 29–30, 42, 57–58
Giles, Capt. Fred A. 25, 29, 40–41, 59, 104
Goddard, Norman A. 25, 28, 29, 32–34, 62, 74–75
Goebel, Arthur 25, 29, 42–45, 54, 62, 65, 70, 73, 76, 79, 81–85, 88–90, 92–93, 102, 103, 107, 113, 116, 120
Goldsborough, Bryce 69, 70
Grace, Dick 16, 18–20, 43
Grieve, McKenzie 4
Griffin, Benny 25, 28, 29, 30–32, 34, 42–43, 44, 54, 62, 65, 72, 73, 74, 77

Hawker, Harry C. 4
Hawkins, Lt. Kenneth C. 28, 33, 74–75
Hearst, George 51–52
Hearst, Mrs. George 52
Hearst, William Randolph 32, 51–52, 53, 104, 105, 111, 115

Hegenberger, Lt. Albert F. 16–18, 22, 24, 68
Henley, Al 28, 30–32, 43, 72, 77
Henshaw, George 30
Hickman, Orville 34
Hinton, Lt. Walter 4
Howard, E. 73

Irving, Livingston G. 25, 29, 41, 45, 55, 62, 65, 72, 75, 78
Irving, Madeline 72–73, 78
Irving, S. C. 41

Jay, Ken 50–52, 62, 70, 75–76, 105, 111–112, 114, 115
Jensen, Marguerite (Peg) 15–16, 46, 66, 83, 89, 91, 92, 103
Jensen, Martin 10, 26, 29, 34, 38, 44, 45–47, 55, 58, 59, 61, 62, 64, 65, 66, 73, 76, 80–85, 88, 90–93, 102, 103, 107, 111–112, 116, 120

Kangeter, John H. 23
Keeler, Fred 50
Kelley, Bernard 94, 97, 98–101
Kingsford-Smith, Sir Charles 42
Knope, Lt. Vilas 59–60, 78, 86, 120
Koger, Lt. Cmdr. Easton D. 19

Lagron, Edward 57, 96–97, 99, 100
Lawing, Marvin A. 39, 60, 86, 209
Lederer, Jerome 34, 35
Lemcke, Harvey 10, 25
Lewis, Edwin H. 64
Lincoln, Garland 26
Lindbergh, Charles A. 6–12, 19, 22, 37, 46, 104, 118
Linkins, Henry 18
Lippiott, Cecil 43–44
Loughead, Alan 50
Loughead, Malcolm 50
Lowes, Marilyn 36
Lowes, Ralph C. 28, 35–37, 57, 60, 62, 71, 94–96, 98–101
Lundgren, Ted 29–30, 42, 57–58
Lunt, George A. 4

MacConaughey, Harry E.   23, 108
Maitland, Lt. Lester J.   16–18, 22, 24, 68
Malloska, W. F. "Bill"   37–39, 63, 66, 79, 104
Martin, Lt. Robert   98
McComb, Lt. Cmdr. M. B.   23, 89
McCracken, William P.   96, 119
McGonagle, W. C.   12
Mdivani, Prince Serge   16
Merrill, Prof.   51
Mitchell, Ed   16
Mitchell, Gen. Billy   8
Mix, Tom   8
Moffett, Edmond   17
Morgan, C. W. F.   4
Morrow, John   103
Mosher, Capt.   100

Negri, Pola   16
Noble, George   100
Northrop, Jack   50, 51, 52, 56, 62, 70, 75–76
Noville, Lt. George   100
Nungesser, Capt. Charles   6, 8

Olwiera, J. Jr.   103
Orteig, Raymond   5, 6
Osborne, Cuzon   26

Palmer, Capt. Burdette A.   72
Parker, Billy   30, 44–45, 54, 69–70, 73, 79, 83, 107
Parkhurst, Charles W.   25, 28, 29, 34–37, 57, 61, 62, 63, 71, 94–96, 98–101
Parkin, Walter   55
Parente, Anthony   17
Pawlikowski, Leo P.   48
Pedlar, John A. (Augy)   16, 25, 28, 29, 37–39, 59–60, 63, 71, 76, 77, 78–79, 86–87, 103, 104, 120
Petrie, G. J.   18
Phillips, Frank   30, 44
Phillips, Jerry   42
Pickford, Mary   8
Pogue, Coville   103
Powell, Virginia   56

Raynham, Capt. F. P.   4
Read, Lt. Cmdr. Albert C.   4
Redfern, Paul   16
Rhodes, Eugene S.   4
Rickenbacker, Eddie   8
Rochlen, A. M.   51–52, 115
Rodd, Ens. Herbert C.   4
Rodgers, Cmdr. John   5, 23, 64
Rogers, Capt. Arthur V.   25, 29, 50, 59–60, 120
Rogers, Mary Louise   60
Romkey, Glenn J.   34, 37, 98

Schalski, Rose Anne   13
Scheetz, Lt. Cmdr. W. H.   18
Schluter, Paul   55, 59, 61, 62, 73, 76, 80–85, 90–92, 112, 120
Schoenhair, Lee   83, 87, 102
Scott, Denham   70, 105, 111–116
Scott, Gordon   29, 51, 53, 56, 62, 70, 73, 75, 83, 87, 105, 113–116, 120
Scott, Shelia   73, 114
Scott, Will   67
Shorey, C. F.   9
Sloniger, Windy   37–38
Smith, Capt. L. H.   23
Smith, Ernest L.   16–18, 20–21, 22, 30, 85, 100
Smith, Ruby   61
Sounders, C. W.   23, 108
Spangenberger, Carl   19
Stanz, Otis   5
Starbuck, Art   55, 96, 100
Stone, Lt. Elmer   4

Tannus, S. F.   34–37, 57, 60–61, 63, 71, 94, 96, 97, 98, 101
Tower, Capt. John   105
Tracey, M. E.   120

Vance, Claire K.   16, 46
Van Valkenburg, A. W.   23

Waggener, Lt. Richard   29, 48–49, 56, 120
Warren, Jeff   29, 48
Weill, Lawrence   29–30, 42, 57–58

Wellman, Walter 4
Welty, M. W. 44
Wilbur, Curtis D. 33, 119
Wilhelm, Miss 103
Wilkins, Hubert 111
Wood, R. E. 17

Wooley, R. E. 12
Wooster, Lt. Stanton 6
Work, Hubert 9
Wyatt, Lt. Ben 55, 59, 61, 100, 108

Young, Clarence W. 9, 59, 69